To build a more sustainable, equitable and democratic world, we need an empowered, connected and durable movement of citizens. We cannot build this kind of movement through appeals to people's fear, greed or ego. As this handbook outlines, such motivations tend to produce shallow, short-lived types of engagement. They are also likely to backfire, actually reinforcing values that undermine social and environmental concern.

How, then, do we go about finding solutions to the most important problems facing us—widespread and persistent poverty, climate change, isolation and loneliness, human rights abuses, inequality, biodiversity loss? The power of protest and popular struggles has been proven time and again, in countering vested interests, and in bringing about new political and social structures. But what are the values that either promote or inhibit these movements? What values help create today's social norms and institutions, and what, in turn, shapes these values?

Fostering "intrinsic" values—among them self-acceptance, care for others, and concern for the natural world—has real and lasting benefits. By acknowledging the importance of these values, and the "frames" that embody and express them; by examining how our actions help to strengthen or weaken them; and by working together to cultivate them, we can create a more compassionate society, and a better world.

After a quick introduction *(pg. 5)* and discussion of what values are (guiding principles based on what people think is important), we're going to talk about why values matter *(pg. 8–9)*. There are many other things that influence any human being in individual moments and across entire lifespans, but our values are a guiding force—abstract ideals (such as equality, tradition, wealth, creativity) that shape our thoughts and actions. This means they influence important aspects of our lives, such as how we vote, what we buy, our choice of friends, and how happy we are.

Research supports some fairly commonsense observations of how values work *(pg. 12–21)*. Some values are compatible, likely to be held strongly together; others—wealth and equality, for instance—not so much. But the research also shows that even in simply talking to one value, you find yourself talking to a range of related values and suppressing the opposing ones. This means, worryingly, that if you've tried to get people to care more about equality by appealing to their desire for popularity, you might have accidentally harmed your own cause.

Humans use values *(pg. 24–27)* to guide behaviour, then—but there are contextual and habitual reasons which mean that not all our behaviours are in line with our values. We also use values as guiding standards, for instance in making judgements—and one result of this is that we find it weird when we're presented with something that seems to convey conflicting values strongly.

We're then going to look at how values change *(pg. 30–31)* and how values have shifted in the past *(pg. 32–33)*. Throughout our lives, we experience opportunities for, and constraints on, the development of specific values. We might learn to value tradition while watching history documentaries, or to want social recognition from reading gossip pages in the tabloids. There are also bigger things that have an impact—large societal or economic changes that make us more concerned about different things.

The values we develop affect how we look at the world. This is partly through frames *(pg. 36–39)*, which are bundles of associated knowledge and ideas in our memories. 'Framing' is also an important tool in communicating—and refers to the information and underlying values we leave in or out when conveying a message.

All of these insights have implications *(pg. 42–53)* for the work of those wanting to bring about lasting changes in the world. We're going to lay out some guiding principles *(pg. 44–47)* to help align our actions with our values, see the bigger picture, think about the values we're all endorsing, and work together more; some specific thoughts about the areas in which we are working for change *(pg. 48–51)* and some thoughts on different spaces for *(pg. 52)* and degrees of change *(pg. 53)* in using this approach. These will be useful for creating campaigns, organising community events, teaching and learning, improving sustainable business practice and policy, and more. We've put in some examples (mostly from the third sector—reflecting our own bias!) of where we think this kind of approach is already being done well. And we finish with some FAQs *(pg. 58–63)* and some thoughts on what to do next *(pg. 54–55)*.

We've developed a workshop to familiarise, engage, and start conversations with groups on all of this. In the back of this handbook, you'll find a set of exercises *(pg. 66–73)* to carry out yourself, individually or in a group, based on the workshop. You'll be pointed to them in the main text. We have found them useful in getting a grasp on the concepts and we recommend doing them—go get a pen!

If you've only got five minutes, read the guiding principles *(pg. 44–47)* and then skip to the FAQs *(pg. 58–63)*.

Finally, go and visit the website valuesandframes.org—it's nice.

ACKNOWLEDGEMENTS

We'd like to thank the following people for their invaluable assistance in shaping this handbook—for their comments, thoughts and many insightful ideas—and for the hours of fascinating conversations we've had with them:

Jon Alexander / Tim Baster / Guppi Bola / Andy Brown / Adrian Cockle / Tom Crompton / Amy Dartington / David Rennie / Matt Downie / Maurice Frankel / Ed Gillespie / Becks Gowland / Anna Grigoryeva / Tanya Hawkes / Chris Johnes / Tim Kasser / Martin Kirk / Casper ter Kuile / Tom Lickiss / Peter Lipman / Charles Medawar / Greg Maio / George Marshall / Charlotte Millar / Amy Mount / Morgan Phillips / Michael Narberhaus / David Norman / RachelNunn / Alex Randall / Ro Randall / Rupert Read / Hetan Shah / Shilpa Shah / Guy Shrubsole / Neil Sinden / Tom Stafford / Esther Tew / Dan Vockins / Adeela Warley / Robin Webster / Katie Welford / Josie Wexler / Christopher Zealley

We'd also like to thank the Society for Participation, Engagement, Action and Knowledge Sharing for facilitating input from social justice activists based on a critical reading of an early draft of the report.

Finally, we'd like to thank the hundreds of workshop participants who were guinea pigs for our draft versions of the handbook; we're sorry we don't have space to name you all individually!

Responsibility for any errors, omissions or mistakes lies solely, of course, with PIRC.

This handbook builds on the initiative of a group of staff from COIN, CPRE, Friends of the Earth, Oxfam and WWF-UK, who published Common Cause: The Case for Working with our Cultural Values, in September 2010. This group has since been extended to include many other organisations, including Action for Children, Cambridge Carbon Footprint, the new economics foundation and Think Global. If you are interested in joining this group, and contributing to its future work, please do get in touch through our website, valuesandframes.org

The world faces some big and serious problems. Globally, progress towards achieving quality of life indicators has been limited, with over a billion people continuing to live in extreme poverty.[1] The future of international action on climate change seems uncertain. Damage and degradation of ecosystems across the world is serious, widespread and ongoing.[2] Here in the UK economic inequality recently reached a 50-year high,[3] child wellbeing is the lowest-ranked in the developed world[4] and anti-immigrant and Islamophobic sentiment have become widespread[5]—as has disengagement from social justice issues.[6]

Encouraging headway continues to be made in many areas, and the progress achieved—and damage prevented—are undoubtedly important. Yet these challenges reflect systemic, structural problems that remain stubbornly intact, in spite of many efforts to spur lasting change. The power of vested interests and the inertia of entrenched political institutions have frequently prevented major inroads being made.

However, one of the most neglected factors in pushing for change is the set of values that motivate people—which represent a strong driving force behind many of our attitudes and behaviours. Examining these values more closely reveals some deep connections between seemingly different issues —and a wealth of opportunities to bring about lasting, systemic change.

Go to page 64 for Exercise 1.

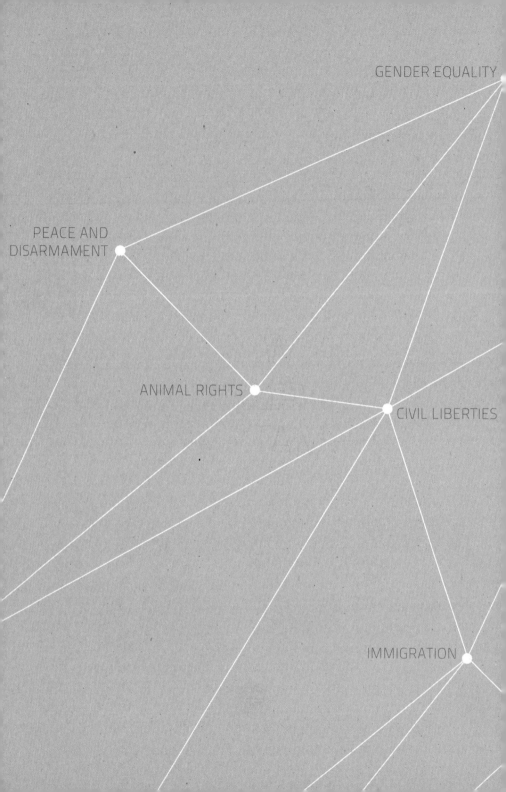

GENDER EQUALITY

PEACE AND
DISARMAMENT

ANIMAL RIGHTS

CIVIL LIBERTIES

IMMIGRATION

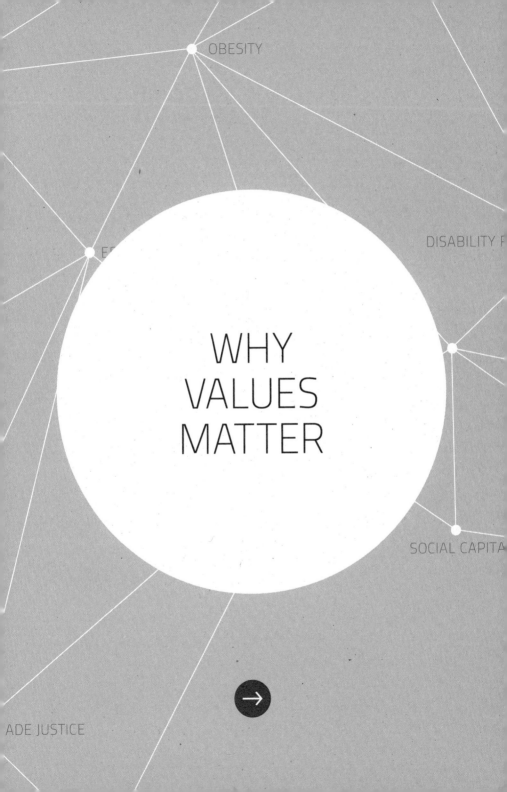

OBESITY

DISABILITY

WHY
VALUES
MATTER

SOCIAL CAPITA

ADE JUSTICE

→

Values represent our guiding principles: our broadest motivations, influencing the attitudes we hold and how we act.

In both action and thought, people are affected by a wide range of influences. Past experience, cultural and social norms, and the money at our disposal are some of the most important. Connected to all of these, to some extent, are our values—which represent a strong guiding force, shaping our attitudes and behaviour over the course of our lives. Our values have been shown to influence our political persuasions; our willingness to participate in political action; our career choices; our ecological footprints; the amount of resources we use, and for what purpose; and our feelings of personal wellbeing.[7]

OUR INTERESTS

OUR LEVELS OF CONCERN
ABOUT GLOBAL CONFLICT

OUR ATTITUDES
TOWARDS GAY RIGHTS

HOW NATIONALISTIC
WE ARE

OUR POLITICAL
PERSUASIONS

HOW CONCERNED WE ARE
ABOUT ENVIRONMENTAL
DAMAGE

OUR LEVELS OF
MILITARISM AND
PEACEFULNESS

OUR LEVELS OF
CONCERN ABOUT
GLOBAL POVERTY

OUR ATTITUDES
TOWARDS HUMAN
RIGHTS

OUR ATTITUDES
TOWARDS
IMMIGRATION

HOW MUCH WEIGHT
WE PLACE ON
BEHAVING MORALLY

OUR LEVELS OF SUPPORT
FOR ENVIRONMENTAL
POLICIES

WHETHER, AND HOW FAR
WE THINK COMPANIES
SHOULD BE ACCOUNTABLE
FOR THEIR SOCIAL AND
ENVIRONMENTAL IMPACTS

HOW FAR WE BELIEVE
IN PUNISHING OR
REHABILITATING
CRIMINALS

OUR LEVELS OF SEXISM,
RACISM AND GENERAL
PREJUDICE TOWARDS
'OUT-GROUPS'

HOW MUCH WE WORRY
AND ARE MOTIVATED
TO FIND OUT ABOUT
'BIG ISSUES'

↑ Figure 1. Various ways that values
influence attitudes and behaviours.[8]

Social and environmental concern and action, it turns out, are based on more than simply access to the facts[9] (a finding that may seem obvious, but has often proven difficult to fully acknowledge). In reality, both seem to be motivated above all by a particular set of underlying values. In what follows, we will examine what values are (and what they are not), the ways they work in a dynamic and interacting system, and why they are so important for those concerned with social and environmental issues.

Go to page 64 for Exercise 2.

VALUES
CAN SEEM ABSTRACT,
BUT THEY HAVE BEEN
SHOWN TO INFLUENCE
MANY OF OUR:

ATTITUDES (PAGE 8)

BEHAVIOURS (PAGE 9)

OUR ECOLOGICAL
FOOTPRINTS

HOW EMPATHIC
WE ARE

HOW MUCH WE
RECYCLE

HOW WE VOTE

HOW MUCH WE
WALK OR CYCLE

THE TYPE OF CAREER
WE CHOOSE

WHAT WE EAT

HOW MUCH WE
PICK UP OTHER
PEOPLE'S LITTER

HOW MUCH WE
VOLUNTEER
TO HELP OTHERS

HOW MUCH WE
CONSERVE
ELECTRICITY

WHETHER, AND HOW
FAR, WE GET INVOLVED
IN POLITICAL ACTIVISM

OUR PURCHASING
DECISIONS, HOW MUCH
WE SPEND, AND ON WHAT

WHETHER, AND HOW
FAR, WE BEHAVE
ALTRUISTICALLY

WHETHER, AND HOW
CONSISTENTLY, WE BUY
'ETHICAL' PRODUCTS

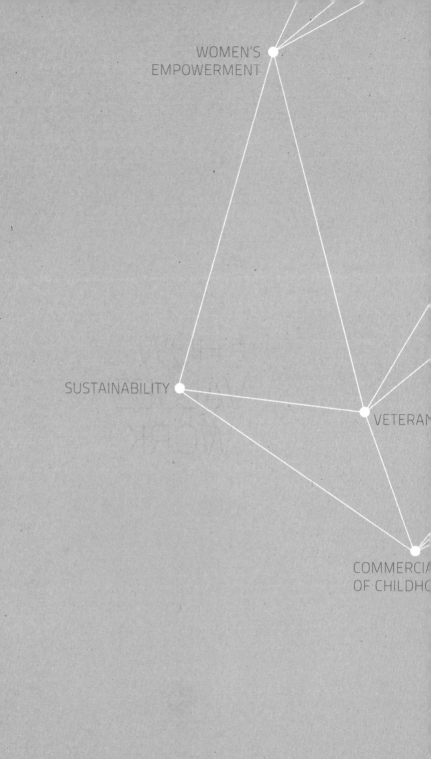

WOMEN'S
EMPOWERMENT

SUSTAINABILITY

VETERAN

COMMERCIA
OF CHILDH

IMMIGRATION

TRADE JUSTICE

RE

HOW
VALUES
WORK

Following decades of research and hundreds of cross-cultural studies, psychologists have identified a number of consistently-occurring human values.[10]

Early researchers into human motivations discovered a surprising consistency in the things people said they valued in life. After testing this finding many times and across many countries and cultures, they put together a list of repeatedly occurring values.[11]

Go to page 66 for Exercise 3.

Rather than occurring randomly, these values were found to be related to each other. Some were unlikely to be prioritised strongly at the same time by the same individual; others were often prioritised strongly at the same time.[12]

The researchers mapped this relationship according to these associations, as presented opposite. The closer any one value 'point' is to another, the more likely that both will be of similar importance to the same person. By contrast, the further a value is from another, the less likely that both will be seen as similarly important. This does not mean that people will not value both cleanliness and freedom, for example —rather, they will in general tend to prioritise one over the other. Values can thus be said to have neighbours and opposites.[13] Based on these patterns of association—as well as their broad similarities —they were then classified into ten groups.

→ Figure 2. Statistical analysis (dimensional smallest space analysis) of value structure across 68 countries and 64,271 people.

See page 68–69 for full definitions.[14]

[How do your answers to Exercise 1 relate to this?]

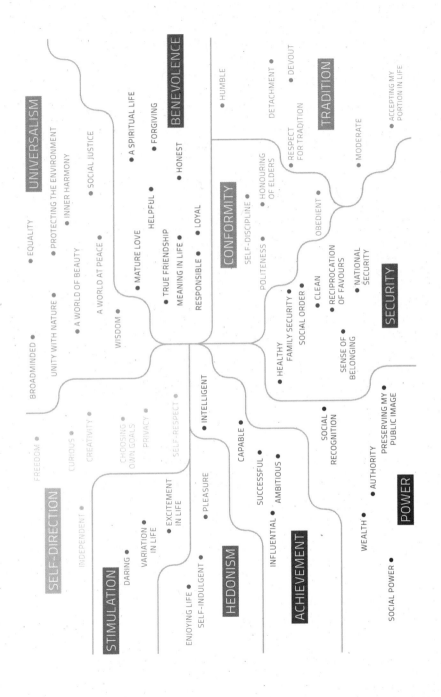

The ten groups are described as follows:

UNIVERSALISM
UNDERSTANDING, APPRECIATION, TOLERANCE
AND PROTECTION FOR THE WELFARE OF ALL
PEOPLE AND FOR NATURE.

BENEVOLENCE
PRESERVATION AND ENHANCEMENT OF THE
WELFARE OF PEOPLE WITH WHOM ONE IS IN
FREQUENT PERSONAL CONTACT.

TRADITION
RESPECT, COMMITMENT AND ACCEPTANCE OF
THE CUSTOMS AND IDEAS THAT TRADITIONAL
CULTURE OR RELIGION PROVIDE THE SELF.

CONFORMITY
RESTRAINT OF ACTIONS, INCLINATIONS AND
IMPULSES LIKELY TO UPSET OR HARM OTHERS
AND VIOLATE SOCIAL EXPECTATIONS OR NORMS.

SECURITY
SAFETY, HARMONY, AND STABILITY OF SOCIETY,
OF RELATIONSHIPS, AND OF SELF.

↑ Table 1. Definitions of the ten values groups.[15]

POWER
SOCIAL STATUS AND PRESTIGE, CONTROL OR
DOMINANCE OVER PEOPLE AND RESOURCES.

ACHIEVEMENT
PERSONAL SUCCESS THROUGH DEMONSTRATING
COMPETENCE ACCORDING TO SOCIAL STANDARDS.

HEDONISM
PLEASURE AND SENSUOUS GRATIFICATION
FOR ONESELF.

STIMULATION
EXCITEMENT, NOVELTY AND CHALLENGE IN LIFE.

SELF-DIRECTION
INDEPENDENT THOUGHT AND ACTION—CHOOSING,
CREATING, EXPLORING.

These groups can be represented more simply in a circular diagram, called a circumplex:

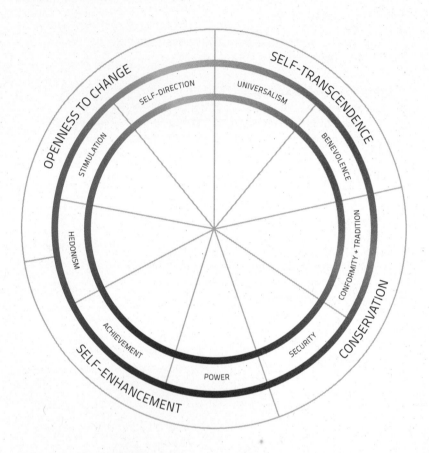

↑ Figure 3. Schwartz's value circumplex.[16]

The ten groups of values can then be divided along two
major axes, as shown above:

1 **Self-enhancement** (based on the pursuit of personal status and
success) as opposed to **self-transcendence** (generally concerned
with the wellbeing of others);

2 **Openness to change** (centred on independence and readiness
for change) as opposed to **conservation** values (not referring to
environmental or nature conservation, but to 'order, self-restriction,
preservation of the past and resistance to change').

Much of the ongoing research on values simply supports some
commonsense, intuitive ideas. Some values or motivations are likely
to be associated; others less so. When we are most concerned for
others' welfare, we are very unlikely to be strongly interested in our
own status or financial success (and vice versa). When we are at our
most hedonistic or thrill-seeking, we are unlikely simultaneously to
be strongly motivated by respect for tradition. But it also reveals
that these relationships are not unique to our culture or society.
They seem to recur, with remarkable consistency, all over the world.

Features of values
Some of the most important features of values are summarised below:

Values are universal
The circumplex is not an astrological chart, and values are not character types. Each of us is motivated by all of these values, but to differing degrees.

Engaging values
Values can be temporarily 'engaged,' when brought to mind by certain communications or experiences—and this tends to affect our attitudes and behaviours. When reminded of benevolence values, for instance, we are more likely to respond positively to requests for help or donations.[17] Our values therefore not only change at different points of our lives, but also day-to-day.

The bleedover effect
Values that appear next to each other on the circumplex are more likely to be prioritised to the same extent by a person. Moreover, when one value is temporarily engaged, it tends to 'bleed over,' strengthening neighbouring values and associated behaviours.

This relationship can produce some surprising results. People reminded of generosity, self-direction and family, for example, have been found to be more likely to support pro-environmental policies than those reminded of financial success and status— without any mention of the environment being made.[18]

The see-saw effect
Whereas neighbouring values are compatible, values on opposite sides of the circumplex are rarely held strongly by the same person. When one value is temporarily engaged, opposing values (and behaviours associated with them) tend to be suppressed. As with a see-saw, when one value rises, the other tends to fall.

This has been illustrated consistently in experiments; for instance people asked to sort words related to achievement values (such as 'ambition' and 'success') from other words were less likely to volunteer their time to help a researcher (a behaviour associated with benevolence values).[19]

Values aren't characteristics

While the terms used to describe values are often also used in everyday speech to describe characteristics or outcomes, it's important to distinguish between the two. While there may well be a correlation between some motivations and seemingly related outcomes, this is by no means always the case. Pleasurable activities are not necessarily motivated by hedonism (you can experience pleasure while pursuing any of your values), while a powerful social movement may be motivated more by social justice and equality (universalism values) than by power. There is even some evidence that artists motivated by their work— rather than by fame, rewards, or a desire to 'prove themselves' —ultimately tend to be the most successful.[20] In this and similar cases, achievement as a motivation can hinder achievement as an outcome.

It's also important to be clear about the—often quite specific— definitions of each of these values. Desiring 'achievement' in the sense of 'personal success through demonstrating competence according to social standards,' for instance, is quite different from a desire to 'achieve' advances for equality, world peace or environmental protection (all universalism values).

See page 66–67 for full definitions.

Values and goals

Our values are related to our goals—another way of measuring and categorising the things we strive for in our lives. Goals can also be grouped on a circumplex according to the compatibilities and conflicts between them.[21] Two of these groupings—intrinsic and extrinsic—are particularly important, and have also been found to recur across cultures.[22]

The distinction between intrinsic and extrinsic goals is similar to that between self-transcendence and self-enhancement values. The two categorisations are not completely interchangeable, but for the sake of simplicity we will combine the two concepts into 'intrinsic values' and 'extrinsic values.' Extrinsic values are centred on external approval or rewards; intrinsic values on more inherently rewarding pursuits.

INTRINSIC

VALUES THAT
ARE INHERENTLY
REWARDING TO PURSUE

EXAMPLES

AFFILIATION TO FRIENDS & FAMILY
CONNECTION WITH NATURE
CONCERN FOR OTHERS
SELF-ACCEPTANCE
SOCIAL JUSTICE
CREATIVITY

EXTRINSIC

VALUES THAT ARE
CENTRED ON EXTERNAL
APPROVAL OR REWARDS

EXAMPLES

WEALTH
MATERIAL SUCCESS
CONCERN ABOUT IMAGE
SOCIAL STATUS
PRESTIGE
SOCIAL POWER
AUTHORITY

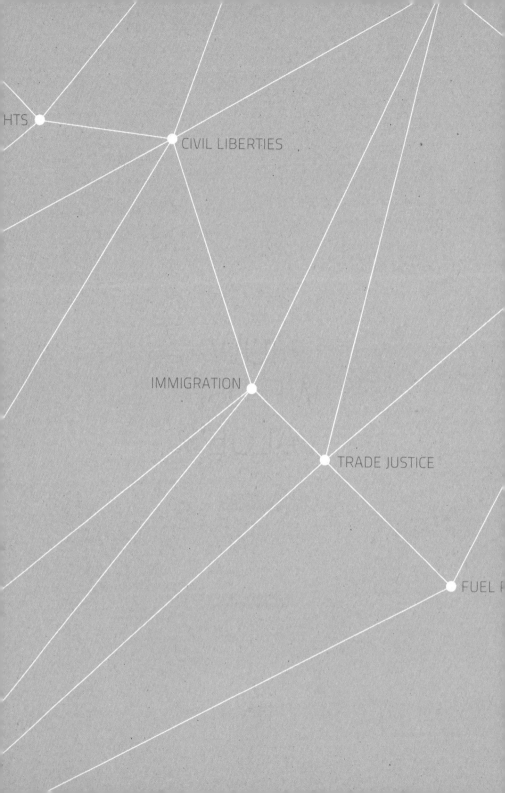

COMMUNITY

HIV/AIDS

WELL-

HOW
WE USE
VALUES

Different values, and the psychological relationships between them, have important effects on our behaviours and attitudes. Some of them reveal a deep connection between many of the issues we work on. However, other factors (contextual, environmental, and habitual) play a role too—suggesting that it is still important to address structures and policies.

Values and the issues we face

Prioritising intrinsic values such as freedom, creativity and self-respect (self-direction values), or equality and unity with nature (universalism values) is closely related to political engagement,[23] concern about social justice,[24] environmentally-friendly behaviours,[25] and lower levels of prejudice.[26]

In contrast, placing more importance on extrinsic values is generally associated with higher levels of prejudice;[27] less concern about the environment and corresponding behaviours;[28] weak (or absent) concern about human rights;[29] more manipulative behaviour[30] and less helpfulness.[31]

What motivates us also seems to affect our levels of wellbeing. Extrinsic values—such as wealth, or preservation of public image—tend to undermine our levels of personal wellbeing.[32] In general, the esteem of others or pursuit of material goods seem to be unreliable sources of satisfaction in life. Other, more inherently rewarding pursuits—such as those found in intrinsic motivations and self-direction values—seem to provide a firmer foundation.[33]

It is common to see people segmented into distinct groups or dichotomies (right/left, for/against, good/bad). The evidence, however, suggests that people are far more complex than this and are unlikely to subscribe purely to one set of values or another. Rather, everyone holds all of the values, and goals, but places more importance on some than others. Each of the values will therefore have an impact on any individual's behaviour and attitudes at different times.

Values are an important driver of behaviour
(but there are other factors at work too)

Our values, then, are strongly related to various kinds of behaviour. People who hold tradition values strongly are more likely to observe national holidays and customs.[34] Stronger achievement values are associated with stress-related behaviours (such as taking on too many commitments); stronger hedonism values with over-eating.[35]

It is clear, however, that values are not the sole determinant of our behaviour: in fact, our actions can at times be fairly divergent from our dominant values. The failure of witnesses to intervene in emergencies— such as an act of violence or an accident—is one well-known example.[36] Equally, though we may hold pro-environmental and pro-social values, we might not always act in ways that would protect either people or the environment (we might not always buy organic or fairtrade produce, for example).[37] A highly intrinsically-oriented person may also be motivated at times by extrinsic rewards such as personal recognition.

Research supports some fairly commonsense explanations for this gap between values and actions:

For a value to guide a behaviour or attitude, we must see that value as relevant.[38] We may believe in equality for women, for example, but fail to recognise this value as relevant in our responses towards other groups.[39]

A value must not be in competition with another value that is more strongly held, more strongly engaged, or seen as more relevant at the time.[40]

Context and social norms are also important. We are far more likely to act in certain ways if those around us are doing the same, or if it is the 'expected' behaviour (particularly if we value conformity highly).[41]

Our level of control also matters. There are times when we are powerless to help another person or find that we have to overcome enormous obstacles in order to make the right choices. If our council does not provide facilities for recycling, a decent transport service, or safe roads for cycling, then these green behaviours will be difficult to sustain (though these constraints will also be in part a product of the values that are dominant in society).[42]

Clearly, then, various aspects of our society may constrain people from expressing the intrinsic values they hold. Education, the media, and social pressures are likely to influence the kinds of values seen as relevant to particular situations—and the normalisation of consumer culture will shape social norms and expected behaviours. Equally, large levels of personal debt will significantly constrain people's scope for action.

We use values in making judgements.
Again, although there are other factors at play, the judgements we make are often related to our values: whether we support a political party or policy, or what media we engage with. The relationship between values has an important effect on our judgements. Because of the tension between them, when opposing values are engaged at the same time, we tend to react with conflicting feelings. In the case of anti-terrorism 'security measures,' a person might value both 'freedom,' (a self-direction value), and 'national security' (a security value), experiencing ambivalence when their conflicting attitudes are brought to bear.[43] This has also been shown in some people's ambivalent attitudes towards homosexuality and gay rights,[44] political candidates,[45] minority groups,[46] eating meat,[47] and obesity[48]—where two opposing sets of values pull towards two conflicting attitudes.

This relationship also seems to affect our responses to political rhetoric. People have been shown to find statements referring to compatible values more persuasive than those appealing to opposing values—whether or not they themselves rate the values as important.[49] Similarly, we often react with mixed feelings to people who strongly hold opposing values—even if one is very close to our own, or we approve of both.[50]

Given the impact of values on our responses, it seems useful to look at what influences values themselves, and how they develop and change over time.

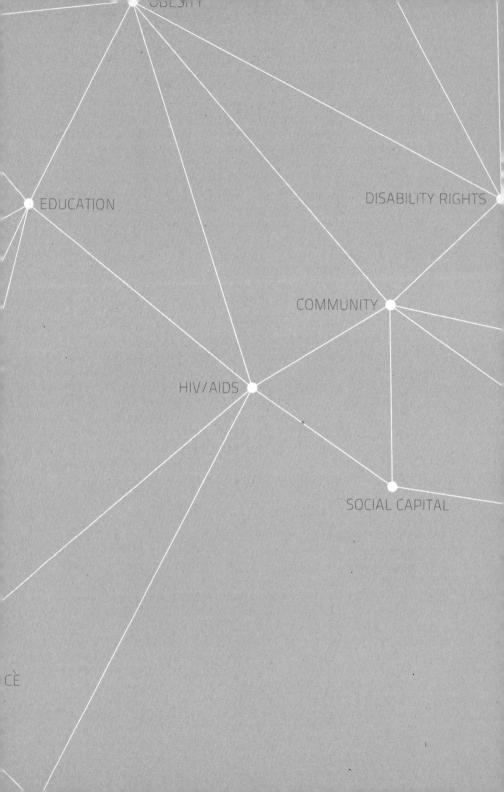

POVERTY

CHIL

HOW
VALUES
CHANGE

WELL-BEING

Each of us holds and is influenced by all of the values listed above, but we differ in how strongly we hold each of them. This in turn is related to how our values have been shaped throughout our lives.

Over time, repeated engagement of values is likely to strengthen them.[51] Our lives therefore provide continual opportunities for—and constraints on—the pursuit and growth of certain values. In addition, experiences themselves are not value-free. A classroom in which the setting is open and accepting of different viewpoints, students are treated as equals, and independence is encouraged may reinforce intrinsic values. In contrast, one which prioritises unquestioning respect for the teacher's authority and is heavy on penalties is likely to engage security, tradition and conformity values. Taking an American law degree appears to cultivate extrinsic values and diminish wellbeing in students during their course of study;[52] and certain types of religious schooling have been shown to cultivate tradition and security values.[53]

Our experience of various aspects of our society will help strengthen particular values. Community centres and churches, trade unions, libraries, local sports clubs—institutions that we share and recognise as promoting the common good —may increase the importance we place on equality, social justice, or friendship. Forests and parks may promote appreciation for nature and other intrinsic values. Extrinsic and security motivations may be strengthened through competitive work environments; advertising appealing to status; the focus of the media on perceived enemies and national security; and the portrayal of financial success as 'achievement' —reflected in rich lists, GDP as the primary indicator of a nation's success, celebrity and fashion culture.

Our experience of particular institutions and policies (themselves shaped in part by societal values) can change or reinforce our perceptions of 'what is possible, desirable and normal':[54] a process known as 'policy feedback.'[55] Anti-discrimination laws, the right to roam, free museums and state pensions may provide opportunities or constraints that promote intrinsic values. Exposure to the institutions of consumer culture may also represent a form of 'policy feedback.' A great deal of commercial advertising and marketing appears to impact upon societal values by promoting materialism and stimulating the desire for security, conformity or self-enhancement.[56] Communications, policies and institutions that embody particular values are likely to have the effect of cultivating those values (and discouraging opposing values) and associated behaviours over time. By playing on people's concern for status and wealth, therefore, we may encourage less environmentally-conscious behaviour and lower concern about other people.

Go to page 68 for Exercise 4.

→ Factors that we and others think are likely (and many
that have been shown) to influence people's values.[57]

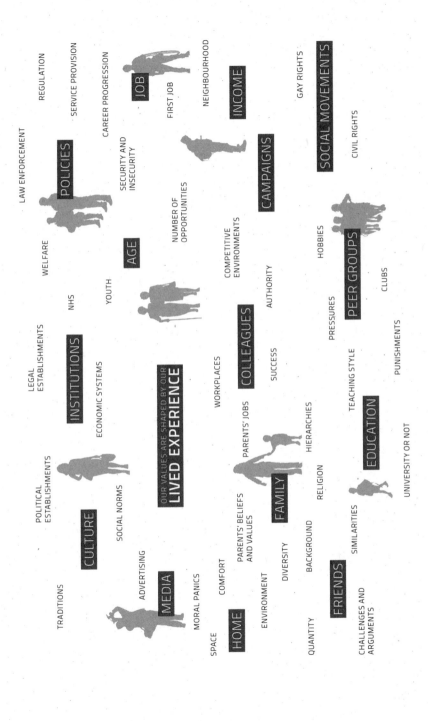

OUR VALUES ARE SHAPED BY OUR
LIVED EXPERIENCE

LAW ENFORCEMENT

REGULATION

SERVICE PROVISION

CAREER PROGRESSION

JOB

FIRST JOB

NEIGHBOURHOOD

INCOME

GAY RIGHTS

SOCIAL MOVEMENTS

CIVIL RIGHTS

POLICIES

SECURITY AND
INSECURITY

CAMPAIGNS

WELFARE

NUMBER OF
OPPORTUNITIES

AGE

YOUTH

COMPETITIVE
ENVIRONMENTS

AUTHORITY

HOBBIES

PEER GROUPS

CLUBS

PRESSURES

NHS

LEGAL
ESTABLISHMENTS

INSTITUTIONS

ECONOMIC SYSTEMS

WORKPLACES

COLLEAGUES

SUCCESS

TEACHING STYLE

PUNISHMENTS

POLITICAL
ESTABLISHMENTS

PARENTS' JOBS

HIERARCHIES

EDUCATION

UNIVERSITY OR NOT

CULTURE

SOCIAL NORMS

ADVERTISING

PARENTS' BELIEFS
AND VALUES

RELIGION

FAMILY

BACKGROUND

DIVERSITY

SIMILARITIES

MORAL PANICS

COMFORT

MEDIA

ENVIRONMENT

HOME

SPACE

TRADITIONS

QUANTITY

FRIENDS

CHALLENGES AND
ARGUMENTS

How values have shifted in the past

Large-scale, widespread changes in values have been observed across the world at different times, and attributed to different factors. In the Czech Republic, the transitional period since communism has seen marked shifts in values—from self-interest and conservation values (encouraged by low levels of social trust and a higher priority placed on conformity) to a much higher significance being placed on intrinsic, universalism and self-direction values.[58] The shift has been attributed to several factors: more young people going to university; the rising use of new technologies, and political discourse that espouses universalism and benevolence values, including 'social justice, equality, peace, environmentalism, honesty, and forgiveness.'[59]

One of the clearest examples of the 'policy feedback' effect in action was the changing attitudes of East Germans towards collective provision of healthcare, welfare and redistribution of wealth in the wake of the reunification of Germany—while those of West Germans remained the same.[60] In a similar way, it has been suggested that Britons' values shifted as a result of the equalising effects of the Second World War—rationing, conscription, the abolition of first class carriages on trains, evacuation, sharing bomb shelters—as well as the subsequent faith in the state's role in the provision of services and a shared ambition to re-build the post-war world.[61]

Other striking shifts in attitudes strongly suggestive of value-change have been noted after particular events. Three years after the introduction of television in Fiji, for example, and during a period of rapid social change, adolescent girls showed a heightened preoccupation with body-image and social competition—attributes directly associated with extrinsic values—and there were dramatic increases in eating disorders.[62] Increases in security values, and decreases in stimulation values, were also documented in children and adults after terrorist attacks, including the Oklahoma bombing, the 9/11 attacks and the London bombings of 2005.[63]

Inevitably, whether they seek it or not, groups can also influence societal values: not only media, but businesses, or political and social movements. Alongside other clear economic and social factors; anti-slavery, women's and labour movements played a significant role in embedding values such as equality and social justice in policy, law and wider society.[64] One study showed that between 1968 and 1971, equality increased in importance from seventh-to third-ranked value among US citizens, and suggests the civil rights movement played an instrumental role in this change.[65] There are also indications that both feminist and Islamist women's groups in Turkey, despite facing continued political, social and religious constraints, have had significant effects on political values and discourse. Their continued promotion of more equal conditions for women, campaigns against domestic violence and struggle for the protection and empowerment of all citizens have had major impacts on laws and attitudes.[66]

It is not difficult to see why all this is likely to be important for our work on the issues we care about. Values influence institutions and norms, and vice versa. Therefore, the values we appeal to; outlets we provide for the expression of different values; and policies we help bring into being will reinforce certain kinds of values, with important effects on people's attitudes and behaviours.

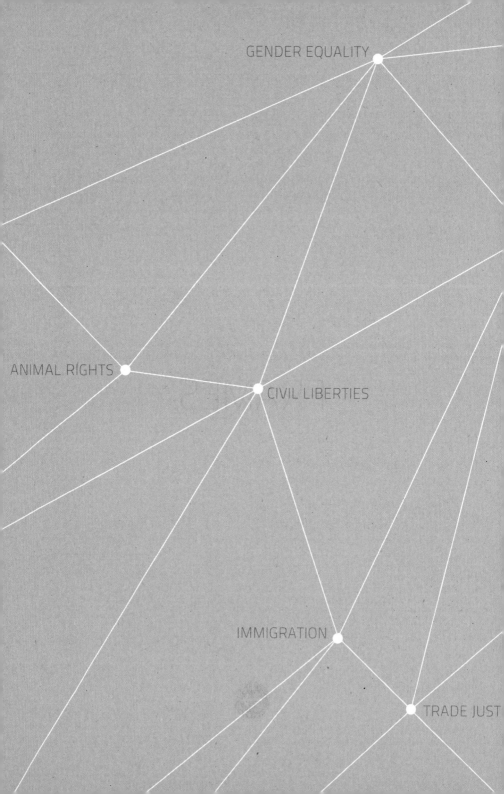

FRAMES

→

Values, as well as influencing our behaviours and attitudes, are connected to the way we understand the world. One way this connection manifests itself is through frames.

Frames are both mental structures that order our ideas; and communicative tools that evoke these structures and shape our perceptions and interpretations over time.[67]

Framing

The frame around a painting or photo can be thought of as a boundary between what has been left in and what has been left out. Each of the elements placed inside the frame is significant, and makes a difference to the meaning of the piece. Similarly, when we communicate about an issue we (consciously or unconsciously) impose boundaries. The emphases, facts and concerns we include can make a real difference to the message conveyed, and to subsequent responses. Support for healthcare reform policies in the US, for instance, was shown to be significantly influenced by whether it was presented as a universal right or a market issue.[68]

The interaction between people, the environment, and the context can also constitute, or evoke, a frame in itself. The way someone responds in an office environment will be different from how they respond in a hospital environment. Frames such as these may be specific to particular contexts or ideas. Other frames are deeper-rooted, broader in scope, and, like ideologies or 'grand narratives,' tend to be applied across a variety of different situations. These often incorporate social or political ideals—such as equality between people, respect for authority, or personal freedom—and are thus strongly connected to our values.

Metaphor

In addition to what we explicitly express, we can also meaningfully frame issues through what we convey implicitly. Metaphor provides a strong and effective tool in framing complex issues quickly. This type of framing often plays an important role in political discourse. Likening national debt to household debt may evoke the idea of a 'united family,' and leads more smoothly to the solution of drastically cutting spending (making 'savings')—omitting issues such as government investment and economic growth.[69]

Frames as associations

Frames reflect associations between concepts, and often values. The *Finding Frames*[70] report explores some of these with reference to the idea of development, which has come to be associated with a particular model of change—which has, in the past, used only economic indicators to judge 'progress.' It documents what they describe as the 'Live Aid legacy,' which relates to the stasis in public perceptions of development in the last 30 years. Mass poverty is thus seen by many as inevitable and unchanging; poor people and countries are poor for reasons inherent to themselves; and the relationship between those in the global, rich north and those in the poor south is implicitly one of powerful giver and grateful receiver. Because of these associations, the term 'charity' tends to normalise and legitimise this unequal power relationship.

The authors suggest these current frames, despite good intentions, risk strengthening extrinsic values such as power, social status and security rather than self-direction and universalism values. Together, these underlying beliefs and values, often subconsciously, seem to be the dominant frame among the UK public for how they understand and respond to initiatives around global development. This inevitably shapes public support for individual giving and government development policy. As an alternative, and amongst other frames, the authors advocate more focus on 'justice,' which has stronger links with intrinsic values.

Reinforcing frames

Over time, frames become embedded in our thinking and discourse through repeated exposure. The frames most prominent in our minds provide communicative shortcuts. These can provide helpful shortcuts or unhelpfully distort our thinking. Frames such as the 'bloated civil service' and 'taxpayers' money' provoke negative reactions to the idea of public spending. An alternative framing might refer to 'public funds.' Frames thus help us define the roles of actors and institutions. Through framing we understand how things work—but also how things *should* work.

Frames as mental structures

Associations between particular words, ideas, emotions and values reflect mental connections that have formed between them over time. Frames, then, are also meaningful 'bundles' of concepts in our minds—gradually learnt through experience and association, strongly linked, and stored in memory. These structures serve as 'frames of reference' for interpreting new information and experience.

We might initially learn about the NHS (the UK's National Health Service) through personal experience with a doctor or at the hospital.

Over time, the NHS will come to be associated with a whole set of such experiences, emotions, and values. Frames will also overlap. An initial 'doctor' frame may become part of a wider 'NHS' frame, a 'welfare state' frame, and an 'expert' frame.Frames, then, are vehicles for engaging and strengthening values. The way we incorporate them in our language, and in the experiences we create and facilitate, are crucially important.

SUPPORT FOR HEALTHCARE REFORM POLICIES
PRESENTED AS A UNIVERSAL RIGHT

SUPPORT FOR HEALTHCARE REFORM POLICIES
PRESENTED AS A MARKET ISSUE

For a more detailed exploration of the issues of frames relevant to social justice and global poverty issues, see *Finding Frames*, which explores, from both a theoretical and practical perspective, the dominant values and frames in discourse on global poverty. It aims to address the growing disengagement from international poverty issues and subsequent lack of substantial action in addressing them.

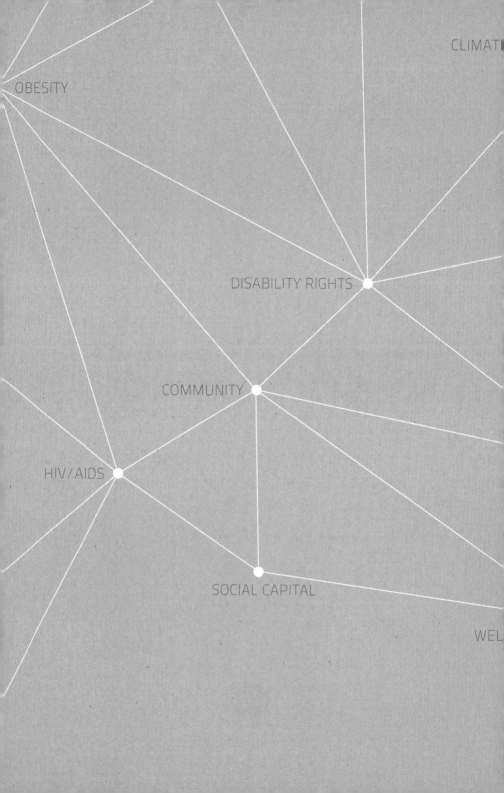

IMPLICATIONS

Working on political and social issues naturally sensitises us to certain dynamics of the world around us—allowing us to recognise the economic or power structures that underpin social behaviours and political institutions. Understanding how values and frames work adds another dimension—opening a range of new avenues for analysis, exploration and intervention.

Values, then, are one important influence on our actions and the way we see the world. Understanding them reveals a major underlying connection between a vast array of major issues—racism, human rights, community welfare, women's empowerment, youth exclusion, biodiversity loss, sustainability. Concern and behaviours related to these problems are all associated with a set of related values.[71] Such an understanding also reveals an important way in which progress on these issues is influenced by education, the media, and other social institutions. Values are engaged and strengthened by our experiences—and we are all a part of each other's experience, whether we like it or not.

It is therefore important to ask what values we want to endorse, and what the implications will be for the issues we care about. The answers to many of these questions may be fairly intuitive, in line with what we currently do, or slot easily into our current areas of activity; others may run counter to our existing practices. Hopefully, however, this understanding will also open up new opportunities for exploration and further work—in how we organise, how we engage with others, and what we call for.

Go to page 73 for Exercise 5.

Collateral damage

One major consideration is that a whole range of our activities are likely to have had important effects we may not previously have acknowledged. One approach that has recently gained ground, for instance, is to tailor communications to appeal to the dominant motivations of different groups of people. Volunteering, educational activities and charitable giving may be presented as opportunities for freebies or personal gain. Environmental behaviour change may be sold via 'eco-chic' for status-conscious people, or opportunities to save cash for the frugal. Similarly, human rights appeals may be 'sold' on the basis that human rights abuses make us (and people like us) less safe.

This approach has helped by highlighting the importance of understanding motivational differences between different groups—and can be successful in achieving some goals. But it is also likely to have brought about significant 'collateral damage.' Because values seem to become stronger with repeated 'engagement,' such appeals are actually likely to reinforce precisely those values that impede lasting change.

Meeting people where they are

Continuing to reinforce extrinsic values in people's motivations is therefore likely to have unintended consequences. At the same time, though, a person's dominant values —which will sometimes be extrinsically-oriented—may well cause them to react negatively to anything seen as directly oppositional to their dominant value-set.

Additionally, the way people express their values may be constrained in particular ways. This may include the normalising of particular behaviours by the media or other institutions, consumer culture, or financial constraints. So even if people prioritise intrinsic values, there may be limited opportunities to pursue related activities where they live or work. A person may believe community and equality are important, but be unfamiliar (and initially uncomfortable) with using democratic processes in the workplace. Equally, people express their values in different ways: some will be used to giving money to causes they care about, others devoting creative time, others simply taking part in discussions.

Meeting people where they are will therefore be important in engaging them, with a view to ultimately creating spaces for change and facilitating the flourishing of more intrinsic values. This means making the most of the shared knowledge and experience we already have on how to initiate and maintain engagement with those around us; thinking about the language and media we use, and the places we work.

Aligning our work with the values that are likely to spur lasting change is clearly unlikely to be a uniformly quick or easy process. Outlined below, however, are some initial guiding principles that will be important in helping us shape our activities in the short, medium and long term.

1 Explore Values

Values and frames open up new avenues for analysis, exploration and intervention: how they are expressed in economic structures, underpin behaviour and institutions, and emerge in our own strategies and practices.

Example: Living Values: A report encouraging boldness in third sector organisations was published in 2006. It explored the values of civil society through a series of workshops in which participants discussed personal and organisational values, such as 'empowering people' and 'transforming lives.' Participants discussed threats to these values (which they agreed came largely from within their organisations) such as top-down organisational approaches and short-termism, and recommended putting values front and centre of all of their activities.

—

bit.ly/livingvalues

2 Nurture intrinsic Values

No aspect of our work is ever entirely value-free, instead both embodying and reinforcing certain values and frames. We should therefore aim not only to promote intrinsic values in communications but to embed them across all areas of our work.

Example: WWF's Natural Change Project 'drew together seven diverse individuals from the business, charitable, arts, public, health and education sectors in Scotland' who were all skilled communicators, and who were described as 'light green.' Through a series of residential workshops and reflective blogging, participants were encouraged to 'think deeply' about sustainability. The experiences appeared to have a profound impact on the participants: who reported having been affected on a deeper level than they had by any more traditional campaign, and had taken away a strengthened connection with nature and sustainability issues more widely, and a desire to share this with others. This resulted in substantial behaviour changes and led them to organise events themselves.

—

bit.ly/naturalchange

3 Challenge extrinsic values

Various elements of our society and culture help foster the desire for wealth, social recognition and power—and simultaneously diminish care for people and the environment. Addressing these will be essential in making progress.

Example: The Equality Trust highlight and campaign to address the detrimental effects of inequality on society. Inequality seems to promote extrinsic values across the population—and not just in poorer groups—by promoting feelings of insecurity, and drives consumerism by cultivating self-enhancing aspirations. These processes drive feelings of stress and anxiety; poor health outcomes such as obesity and heart disease; higher levels of consumption and less sustainable lifestyles.[72] In addition to addressing inequality head on, they identify other points of intervention such as advertising and parts of the media, which play a large role in perpetuating and reinforcing these kinds of values.

—

bit.ly/equalitytrust

4 See the big picture

The benefits of appeals to extrinsic values—in motivating rapid or significant policy changes—may occasionally outweigh the 'collateral damage' they cause. Without a clear understanding of values, however, we will not be able to identify and manage these trade-offs effectively. We must not lose sight of the big picture, and a vision of long-term, systemic change, with a clear understanding of the values that will underpin it.

Example: The Stern Review on the Economics of Climate Change provides a good illustration of the issue of trade-offs. Its release presented commentators and civil society with a number of relevant concerns to focus on. Many reinforced the dominant framing—concentrating on the purely economic costs of climate change and the economic benefits of addressing it. An alternative frame—many of the features of which were also present in the Stern Review—was available to them, however: a focus on the ethical dimensions, including the negative impacts for people and the natural world. The dominant frame may well have promoted extrinsic values, but also made bigger headlines —bringing more attention to the issues. The alternative may have received less attention, but resisted reinforcing what could be a deeply unhelpful frame—instead encouraging the expression of more intrinsic concerns.

—

For a longer discussion of the Stern Review see: valuesandframes.org/stern

5 Work together

Clearly, no one group or organisation is likely to have much of an impact in shifting values on its own. We need to cooperate and collaborate —both within and across different sectors—to be effective. Because diverse issues are linked by the values that underpin them, we will be continually supporting each other through our efforts.

Example: The Robin Hood Tax has successfully rallied a diverse set of groups, organisations and individuals—including religious groups, big NGOs, smaller civil society organisations, trade unions, economists, and private sector representatives— around the otherwise unlikely cause of financial sector reform. With a clear and strong main message—a levy on financial sector transactions—the campaign has succeeded in drawing together a huge number of causes, from child poverty and public services in the UK to global maternal health and climate change. Importantly, the campaign also draws on a potent frame: the culturally archetypal figure of Robin Hood, who embodies the idea of redistribution as social justice.

—

bit.ly/robinhoodcoalition

There is power in aligning what we say we value and what we show we value. There are likely numerous areas that we work in where reflecting the values we wish to promote would be effective and beneficial to the issues we care about: outlined below are a few thoughts on what these might be.

Communication, education, facilitation

Taking values into account doesn't detract from the importance of the messages we communicate. However, doing so should highlight the values embedded in all aspects of the experience of that message: in the setting, the frames, the level of participation it offers, and the messenger. The type, and depth, of engagement is also significant. A low-involvement experience—reading a leaflet, for instance— is likely to engage with values fairly superficially; while top-down communications may stifle the expression and development of self-direction values. First-hand experience and deeper involvement are likely to have a much greater impact, and self-direction values are more likely to be engaged where self-expression and critical thought are facilitated and encouraged.

Example: Carbon Conversations Groups offer supportive and non-judgemental spaces for people to 'connect, explore and then act on climate change.' Six facilitated group meetings take people through trust-building exercises, discussion and exploration of carbon footprints and lifestyles, and information sharing. The depth of engagement, the openness of the experience, and the encouragement to share and explore the emotional as well as rational responses to the challenges ahead all reflect the intrinsic values embodied in the desire to address environmental issues.

Example: Oxfam's 'Be Humankind' campaign taps into the benevolence value of kindness, while evoking the wider perspective of 'humankind'—aiming to harness and promote intrinsic values more broadly. It also addresses supporters with a call to action as part of a wider human community.

Advocacy, lobbying and policy work

Institutions, policies and social structures play a central role in shaping our lived experience. How can we find out what the full impact of these might be, taking values into account? There are values embedded in the use of economic indicators as a proxy for societal success, for instance. What policies could better embody the appreciation of others and of nature, creativity, and fair opportunities for all?

Example: Mumsnet. The online parenting network Mumsnet have recently sought to counter the objectification of women and the sexualisation of children's culture through campaigns against the marketing of 'lads' mags' and sexualised content to children. These issues are strongly associated with extrinsic values, including power and concern for image,[73] as well as unhealthy behaviours such as eating disorders.[74] Working with a wide variety of actors such as the Archbishop of Canterbury, politicians, health foundations and associations, and the Girl Guides, the campaign has provided a strong and consistent voice on the ethics of these issues. Campaigns such as these may help combat the normalisation of extrinsic values.

Organisation, supporters, finance and fundraising

People's overall experience of organisations will serve to reinforce particular values—and not always those being explicitly promoted. Our relationship with the people we work with can therefore be important. Holding a participatory meeting in a community space embodies very different values from a formal meeting encouraging deference to hierarchical structures. Similarly, financially successful models or techniques often allow limited scope for engagement with those you're working with (and often have a high churn of members, supporters or employees). An example is the civil society model of professionalised 'protest businesses' with direct debits as the deepest level of engagement.[75] What organisational models best embody the values we wish to promote?

Example: The Camp for Climate Action. Participation was embedded in the Camp at a deep level, through national, regional and local decision-making groups. While in practice participation was inevitably limited by factors such as available time, mobility and experience, in principle the decision-making process was open to all, and encouraged direct participation on a horizontal, democratic basis. The human and natural impacts of issues were the focus of discussions, and non-violent, direct and creative action was encouraged.

Example: The fundraising department at the Centre for Alternative Technology have recently started applying a values approach to their work. Firstly, they have begun to foster a culture of non-competitiveness and cooperation, focused on honesty and integrity, both within the department and with other organisations. They have begun removing extrinsic values and frames from both their internal and external communications: for instance, emphasising the work that needs doing, not whether it's 'value for money.' Focus groups have been set up to explore CAT's work, donors' reasons for giving, and ways to deepen donor engagement. Lastly, they are looking at new ways to measure progress, including staff retention and satisfaction, and donor engagement.

Creation and action

Creation and engagement in practical activities, particularly the promotion of creativity for its own sake (and not for rewards or recognition), are often strongly related to self-direction values, which in turn tend to be strongly related to values supportive of social and environmental justice. While many projects embody this ethos and these values already, there may be more points where more people can be encouraged, engaged and included.

Example: Forest Schools aim to 'encourage and inspire through positive outdoor experiences.' Children of all ages regularly visit local woodlands, are given opportunities to learn about the environment and are encouraged to use their own initiative in exploring and problem-solving. Through creating engaging and achievable tasks, Forest Schools aim to promote self-awareness, appreciation of nature, and social and emotional intelligence.

Example: Depave is a US-based organisation which aims to get rid of unnecessary paved areas and create community green spaces in their place. The reasoning is two-fold: concrete, they claim, exacerbates the detachment of people from nature, as well as contributing to storm-water pollution. The recruitment of volunteers is aligned with their mission: only the above reasons are given to encourage applications, and there is no mention of additional reward of any sort. In 2009, 275 volunteers 'depaved' 29,300 square feet of land and created six community green spaces, three sustainable schoolyards, and sixty-five garden plots.

Support and communities

Support and community services could promote self-direction values and be carried out in highly compassionate ways; at other times they may promote conformity, social order, and deference to authority. If the end goal is the care of others (related to intrinsic values), then ensuring the values embodied are aligned with the methods may be important; if not, they may erode the very values and outcomes strived for.

Example: Community Links are an East London group working with disadvantaged communities. Their mission is to "To generate change. To tackle causes not symptoms, find solutions not palliatives. To recognise that we need to give as well as to receive and to appreciate that those who experience a problem understand it best... To distinguish between the diversity that enriches society and the inequalities that diminish it. To grow—but all to build a network not an empire... To never do things for people but to guide and support, to train and enable, to simply inspire." To these ends, they work, embedded in communities, alongside schools, public services and communities themselves. They provide support and advice for gaining skills and employment for adults and youth, child care and play, planting and growing, and other community development; as well as having established a school for excluded students—which succeeded in enabling every student to go on to acquire further skills, education or employment last year. As well as a deep engagement with local issues, they consistently lobby for both national and international policy change.

Example: Friends of the Earth Rights and Justice Team focus on communities 'worst affected by environmental problems and least empowered in decision-making.' Using legal and practical advisers, they engage and give ongoing support and training to these communities. They link the environmental justice issues faced by communities in the UK, such as areas of London, with those faced by those in other parts of the world suffering environmental degradation. Explicit in their actions—bringing forward smaller legal cases and delivering skills training, for instance—is a 'big-picture' perspective, and the goal of addressing wider, more systemic issues. They focus entirely on the human (health and other social) and environmental impacts. The 'justice' frame draws on intrinsic values such as equality and freedom, as well as the legal dimension of the issues they work on.

There are values embedded in how we—as individuals and organisations—interact with each other and the wider world. Below are outlined some thoughts on the implications of this.

How we organise ourselves

The physical spaces and organisational structures we work within are an important part of our lived experience, so it's sensible to ask what values they currently help to strengthen. Do the groups and organisations we are a part of—and the ways we interact with each other—embody the values underpinning our own work?

How we engage with others

The wider world's experience of our organisations —whether through events, services, fundraisers or campaigns—will help to strengthen certain values. Do the messages and experiences we create embody values that are likely to motivate lasting concern about the issues we work on?

What we call for

The changes our groups and organisations work to bring about will have effects beyond those that are more direct or obvious, ultimately serving to strengthen certain values. We must therefore ask what the value impacts of the policies, institutions and practices we advocate will be.

The way we choose to engage with this agenda, and the way we sequence changes, will vary, but can be conceived of as different depths of change.

Building momentum
Mapping and scrutinising the drivers of different values, and starting to work together more. Thinking about new benchmarks for measuring progress and success.

Structural changes
Aligning values across our communications; challenging unhelpful frames. Rethinking our organisations so that the overall experience of them—for employees, leaders, and those we work with—embodies the values we want to promote.

Cementing systemic change
Pushing for policies that foster intrinsic values, and confronting entrenched institutions and norms that reinforce extrinsic values.

We hope that this handbook will be the beginning of a conversation. We certainly don't have all the answers, and we invite you to come and get involved, or provide feedback.

You can also:
→ Attend an event valuesandframes.org/events

→ Request a workshop or hold your own valuesandframes.org/workshop

→ Get together with others to explore this debate further.

→ Start thinking about how your values or those of your organisation align with others.

→ Make some first steps to working with other groups.

→ Join one of the Common Cause working groups valuesandframes.org/ workinggroups

→ Get in touch valuesandframes.org/contact

Or go online and:
→ Read the full Common Cause report valuesandframes.org/downloads

→ Sign up to our newsletter to keep track of the latest work in this area valuesandframes.org/newsletter

→ Share your experience or submit a case study or blog valuesandframes.org/share

→ Or just take a look around, there's a lot going on valuesandframes.org

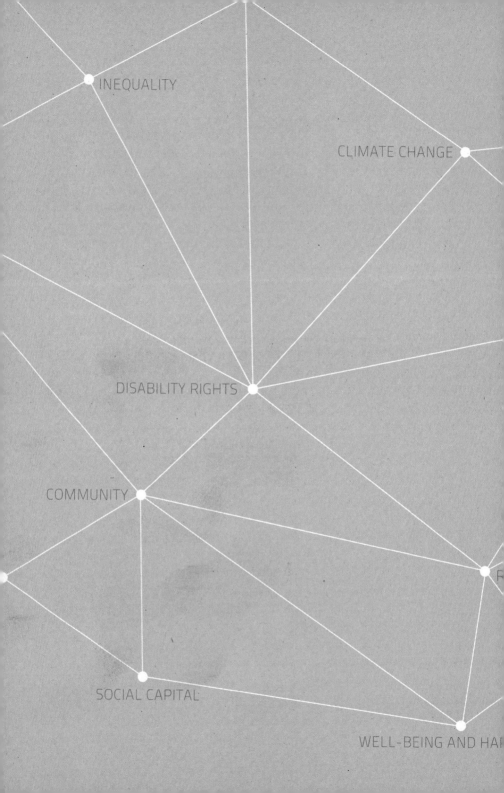

INEQUALITY

CLIMATE CHANGE

DISABILITY RIGHTS

COMMUNITY

SOCIAL CAPITAL

WELL-BEING AND HAI

GAY RIGHTS

GAY

FREQUENTLY ASKED QUESTIONS

BIODIVERSITY LOSS

How robust is the circumplex?
Schwartz built on the research of a social psychologist called Milton Rokeach, who had been carrying out research into values since the 1960s. This body of literature is now well-established and robust. Schwartz's model has been used in thousands of subsequent academic papers (the original article alone has been cited over 3,700 times). Hundreds of papers—amounting to literally 100,000s of participants—have also tested the relationships between the values, using different lab and field methodologies across over 80 countries and in 48 different languages, the vast majority of these papers confirming the relationships Schwartz outlines.

In addition to asking people what they valued, researchers have verified the relationships between values using peoples' friends,' partners' and families' perceptions of their values; [76] and tests to see how easily a value-relevant word is recalled from memory.[77] They have also tested the validity of the model using correlations between behaviours associated with the value sets, such as observing that prioritising tradition and conformity tend to result in similar behavioural tendencies, have some overlap with highly security-driven individuals, and very little overlap with highly stimulation-driven individuals.[78]

The model is also the basis of the values component of the European Social Survey,[79] the largest trans-European social survey, involving almost every national academic funding body in Europe, and collecting data from around 30 countries every two years. The World Values Survey, 'the world's most comprehensive investigation of political and sociocultural change,'[80] also draws on the Schwartz model.

In short, it's pretty robust. That's not to say it is a complete theory of human motivation—rather, it's an approximate but well-founded model of how human values relate to each other, with measurable impacts on our attitudes and behaviours.

Should we try to change people's values—is this ethical?
No campaign, communication, policy or institution is ever value-free. Recognising this—and the impact of values on behaviour—the question instead becomes which values do we want to endorse?

Do we need to change values if we can just change behaviour?
Given the scale and importance of the issues we face, many of us have believed that the ends justify the means. Changing behaviours (or policies) is sometimes seen as key, whatever motivations or methods are harnessed to achieve this goal. The values research, however, suggests that continually compromising on the means risks ultimately placing the desired ends out of reach—by strengthening values that set back efforts towards more systemic change.

Behavioural and policy changes remain important, of course, and we will sometimes need to appeal to extrinsic values to bring them about. An understanding of values simply allows us to place these changes in a broader context—carefully considering the trade-offs we will inevitably face.

Can we have an impact on values? Do we really have the power to do so?
If values are as important as the evidence suggests, we cannot afford not to work to strengthen intrinsic values. Further, although no single group or organisation is likely to have the ability to make much of an impact on values on its own, collaboration within and across different sectors is likely to have a substantial effect.

Do we have the time to shift values?
Some of the issues we face—climate change the prime example—are so urgent that many of us have resorted to ever more desperate short-termist campaigning to spur change. But there is no evidence that these techniques will 'work' at all—let alone in time—since many 'easy wins' can help set back longer-term, more substantial change.

This sounds similar to the approaches of the 1970s—often perceived as 'moral crusades.' Are you saying we should go back to this?
No. These insights from psychological research ought to provide us with new ways of working—a step forwards rather than backwards. Rather than only ever harping on certain topics, we need to find different ways to approach different groups. We should avoid tailoring what we do to appeal to the dominant values of different groups regardless of what these values are, though. Rather, we should find creative, sensitive, intelligent, ways—which may well vary across different groups—to engage the intrinsic values people already hold.

What evidence is there that using extrinsic appeals, or mixing extrinsic and intrinsic appeals, is undermining our work?
Despite the body of evidence that shows that incentives can succeed in increasing participation, response rates, or productivity,[81] there is an increasingly robust case that this only applies to particular contexts. Two strands of literature—from economics and social psychology—have independently reached the same conclusion: offering an extrinsic reward can actually discourage the desired response. The thought of extrinsic reward appears to erode intrinsic motivation, reflecting the see-saw relationship between intrinsic and extrinsic values.

The first academic discussion of this was in the 1970s, when it was suggested that offering monetary rewards decreased the incidence of blood donations.[82] More recently, it was found that—rather than discouraging parents from picking up their children late from day-care—fining them actually increased the number of late arrivals.[83] Studies into giving incentives for volunteering have found that although there is more volunteering when rewards are offered, the amount of time contributed by each volunteer significantly decreases.[84] And schoolchildren given performance incentives collected fewer donations for charity than those not told they would be rewarded.[85]

The conclusions of one of many such studies are illuminating. A referendum was to be held in Switzerland to decide where toxic waste sites should be located, and two researchers carried out a number of large surveys of whether people would be happy to have the waste sites near their own communities.[86] The population was very well informed, and were aware of the risks involved. When the offer of compensation was suggested, 25% of people said yes; without the offer, 50% did. These striking results led the researchers to conclude that thinking about civic responsibility alone was a stronger incentive than thinking about civic responsibility plus money: two motivations which appeared to compete, rather than complement. The intrinsic motivation was clearly present, but the extrinsic focus suppressed it—an effect also known in the literature as 'crowding-out.'

The values research further suggests that the continued encouragement of certain values strengthens them and suppresses or weakens their opposites. Similarly, the lack of opportunity for the expression of certain values will weaken them. This may mean that not only is there a temporary, self-concerned response after an extrinsic appeal, but that the continued use of such appeals will actually strengthen extrinsic values over time, and suppress concern for the wellbeing of others and the environment.

So everything has to be about intrinsic values?
Not necessarily always. The third, private and public sectors are brimming with
expertise on engaging people and effecting change, and this knowledge must be
built on. Values are simply another important element to consider. Techniques used
to engage people in the first instance may be recognisably unhelpful for more sustained
engagement in the longer term; and their impacts on people's values should be carefully
considered. But offering small rewards, such as appealing to people's desire to look
good or to get a free lunch, might be useful in 'getting people in the door'—while the
overall, take-away experience could be centred more on community, creativity or
other intrinsic values.

Are you saying we shouldn't talk about things in economic terms?
This approach does not suggest that any and all talk of questions of cost (say) must
be dispensed with. Rather, we must be careful not to allow these considerations to
dominate our discussions of the advantages and disadvantages of different policies—
as though investment opportunities or the loss to national GDP were the overriding
concerns. Unfortunately this practice has become fairly common, as many groups
have attempted to align their priorities with those of the mainstream media, of
political and economic elites.

Is this just about tweaking communications?
No. A values-based approach requires a 'big picture' perspective: looking at many
more drivers of values and behaviour than simply communications, including policies,
institutions and lived experience more broadly.

Aren't there more important factors in communication than values in any case?
This approach does not advocate throwing out everything else we know about
effective communication (or other aspects of our work). Nevertheless, it does
suggest that alongside and underlying these considerations should be a clearly
thought-out set of values and frames.

This may mean rethinking the way some areas are handled. Since people are
most influenced by those they relate to and respect (including family and peers),
messengers will remain important, for example. But the use of attention-grabbing
celebrity spokespeople may need to be reconsidered—particularly if they are most
closely associated with wealth, social status and other self-enhancement values.

The settings in which we interact with people will also remain important. And we
will still need to present positive visions that engage and inspire. A values-conscious
approach should aim to make these positive visions sustainable, and align them with
values that won't ultimately undermine that vision.

Doesn't this analysis divide values and people into good and bad? Or even left-wing and right-wing?
Values are not 'good' or 'bad' in and of themselves. They are each thought to express different needs, and are therefore each necessary for different purposes. Generally speaking, however, the priority we give to some values relative to others is associated with particular social and behavioural outcomes.

None of us can be considered 'good' or 'bad' as individuals, either. All of us will hold all of the values on the circumplex to some extent. Which of them come to the fore at any given moment will depend on the situation we happen to be in (and this effect will be strengthened over time).

There are a few meaningful associations between values and ideologies, so this connection cannot be entirely dismissed. However, the circumplex cannot simply be mapped onto the political spectrum, and a range of values will inevitably crop up across ideological divisions.[87]

What about speaking to those who are generally motivated by extrinsic concerns?
Everyone holds all of the values on the circumplex, but to differing degrees. Even if a person strongly values power, status or wealth, they will still also hold intrinsic and self-transcendence values. It is therefore possible to engage these values in more extrinsically-oriented people.

Appealing to people with messages highly incongruent with their dominant values can of course sometimes provoke feelings of threat—or simply disinterest—and be dismissed. But sensitivity and creative thinking—particularly in our choices about when, where and how we engage with others—will help us to surmount these barriers.

Are you saying people who have power cannot be intrinsically motivated?
No—and further, leadership and those operating in positions of power can play important roles in pushing for and implementing change. However, an understanding of how values work highlights the significant challenges faced by people in leadership roles—given that there will be constant pressures towards ambition and concern for image or success in attaining and maintaining leadership positions. These challenges are not insurmountable, but they will require self-awareness and reflection on the part of people in leadership roles to overcome them, and they should be supported by critical friends around them.

We have built up relationships with those in positions of power; and we still need to engage those with influence. Aren't appeals to intrinsic values going to alienate them—or simply fall on deaf ears? And doesn't this mean we need to appeal to their existing priorities?

As we have suggested above, because of the distinction between behavioural outcomes and underlying motives and values, a person can have achieved a great deal and be in a position of relative power but be primarily motivated by concern for the wellbeing of others. Even if they are highly extrinsically-oriented or more concerned with power itself, since every person holds every value, they may nevertheless respond to sensitively-pitched appeals to intrinsic values.

Nevertheless, in addressing those within institutions constrained from acting in more intrinsically-motivated ways, some will regard choosing to 'speak their language' (of economic costs and benefits, for instance) as a tolerable trade-off if it helps to secure significant changes.

This approach may sometimes run the risk of causing collateral damage, however. The kinds of appeals with which powerful groups are surrounded may well 'trickle down' through the media. And if policies are rooted in purely economic concerns, the 'policy feedback' they generate may help entrench these values even further. To the extent that we can provide countervailing messages, we may be able to help alter these institutional cultures. Alternatively, we may simply choose not to engage, but rather to try to exert external pressure as a strong popular movement. All these considerations will have to be carefully weighed in such cases.

To read a full list of FAQs, visit valuesandframes.org/faqs

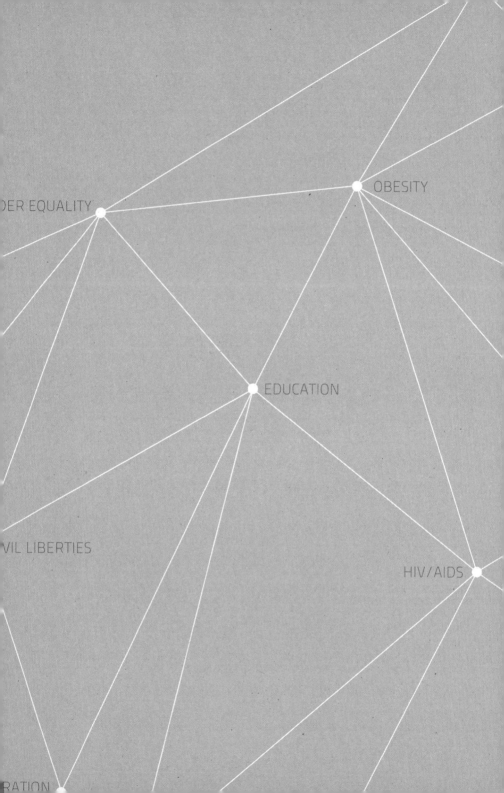

DER EQUALITY

OBESITY

EDUCATION

VIL LIBERTIES

HIV/AIDS

RATION

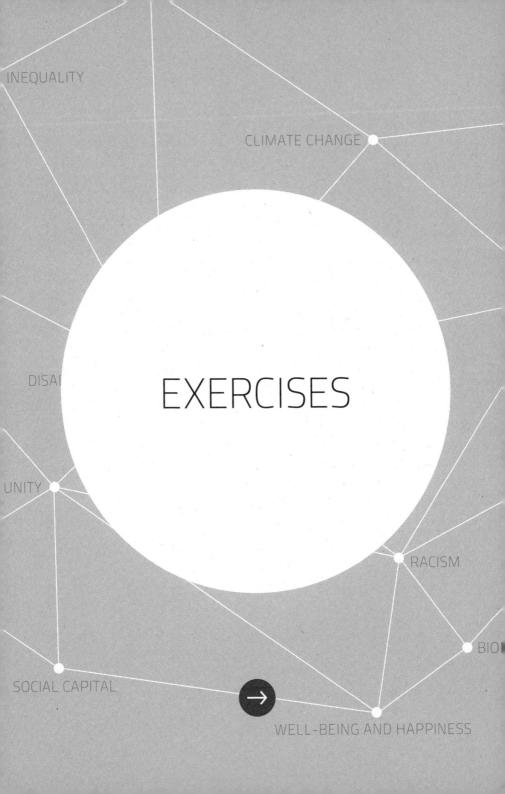

INEQUALITY

CLIMATE CHANGE

DISAB

EXERCISES

UNITY

RACISM

BIO

SOCIAL CAPITAL

→

WELL-BEING AND HAPPINESS

If your organisation or group is interested in holding a workshop, get in touch by visiting valuesandframes.org/workshop: either we can arrange for someone to facilitate or we can provide you with additional materials or advice.

1 **What do you value in life?**
The concepts, ideals, people, places, or things that are important to you.

....

....

....

....

....

....

....

2 **What issues do you care about?**
The issues you think society needs to address, whether in the UK or globally.

....

....

....

....

....

....

3 **What does a society that has addressed these challenges value?**
Imagine a society that had addressed all of the issues you listed in the previous exercise. What would people living in this society value most and what would they value least? Circle the five most important and five least important opposite, using the definitions on the next page.

HUMBLE

DEVOUT

DETACHMENT

PROTECTING THE ENVIRONMENT

INNER HARMONY

A SPIRITUAL LIFE

EQUALITY

SOCIAL JUSTICE

FORGIVING

ACCEPTING MY PORTION IN LIFE

RESPECT FOR TRADITION

HONEST

HONOURING OF ELDERS

MODERATE

A WORLD OF BEAUTY

MATURE LOVE

HELPFUL

LOYAL

SELF-DISCIPLINE

UNITY WITH NATURE

A WORLD AT PEACE

TRUE FRIENDSHIP

MEANING IN LIFE

RESPONSIBLE

POLITENESS

OBEDIENT

BROADMINDED

WISDOM

HEALTHY

FAMILY SECURITY

SOCIAL ORDER

CLEAN

RECIPROCATION OF FAVOURS

NATIONAL SECURITY

FREEDOM

CURIOUS

CREATIVITY

CHOOSING OWN GOALS

PRIVACY

SELF-RESPECT

INTELLIGENT

SENSE OF BELONGING

CAPABLE

EXCITEMENT IN LIFE

PLEASURE

SUCCESSFUL

AMBITIOUS

SOCIAL RECOGNITION

INDEPENDENT

DARING

VARIATION IN LIFE

ENJOYING LIFE

SELF-INDULGENT

INFLUENTIAL

AUTHORITY

PRESERVING MY PUBLIC IMAGE

WEALTH

SOCIAL POWER

A Spiritual Life	Emphasis on spiritual not material matters
A Varied Life	Filled with challenge, novelty and change
A World at Peace	Free of war and conflict
A World of Beauty	Beauty of nature and the arts
Accepting My Portion in Life	Submitting to life's circumstances
Ambitious	Hard working, aspiring
An Exciting Life	Stimulating experiences
Authority	The right to lead or command
Broadminded	Tolerant of different ideas and beliefs
Capable	Competent, effective, efficient
Choosing Own Goals	Selecting own purposes
Clean	Neat, tidy
Creativity	Uniqueness, imagination
Curious	Interested in everything, exploring
Daring	Seeking adventure, risk
Detachment	From worldy concerns
Devout	Holding to religious faith and belief
Enjoying Life	Enjoying food, sex, leisure, etc.
Equality	Equal opportunity for all
Family Security	Safety for loved ones
Forgiving	Willing to pardon others
Freedom	Freedom of action and thought
Healthy	Not being sick physically or mentally
Helpful	Working for the welfare of others
Honest	Genuine, sincere
Honouring of Elders	Showing respect
Humble	Modest, self effacing
Independent	Self reliant, self sufficient
Influential	Having an impact on people and events

Inner Harmony	At peace with myself
Intelligent	Logical, thinking
Loyal	Faithful to my friends, group
Mature Love	Deep emotional and spiritual intimacy
Meaning in Life	A purpose in life
Moderate	Avoiding extremes of feeling & action
National Security	Protection of my nation from enemies
Obedient	Dutiful, meeting obligations
Pleasure	Gratification of desires
Politeness	Courtesy, good manners
Preserving my Public Image	Protecting my 'face'
Privacy	The right to have a private sphere
Protecting the Environment	Preserving nature
Reciprocation of Favours	Avoidance of indebtedness
Respect for Tradition	Preservation of time honoured customs
Responsible	Dependable, reliable
Self Discipline	Self restraint, resistance to temptation
Self Respect	Belief in one's own worth
Self-Indulgent	Doing pleasant things
Sense of Belonging	Feeling that others care about me
Social Justice	Correcting injustice, care for the weak
Social Order	Stability of society
Social Power	Control over others, dominance
Social Recognition	Respect, approval by others
Successful	Achieving goals
True Friendship	Close, supportive friends
Unity with Nature	Fitting into nature
Wealth	Material possessions, money
Wisdom	A mature understanding of life

4 How does lived experience influence values?

What strengthens and weakens some of the values you listed as most important and least important to people living in a society addressing the issues you care about? Think of all the different aspects of lived experience. To help, there's an example below, part-filled with suggestions from some of the workshops we have run.

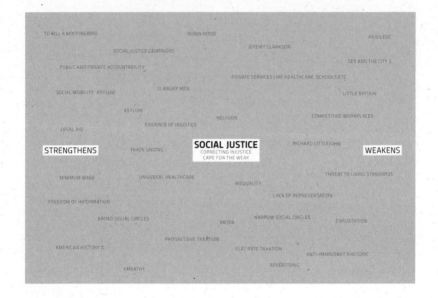

STRENGTHENS   WEAKENS

STRENGTHENS   WEAKENS

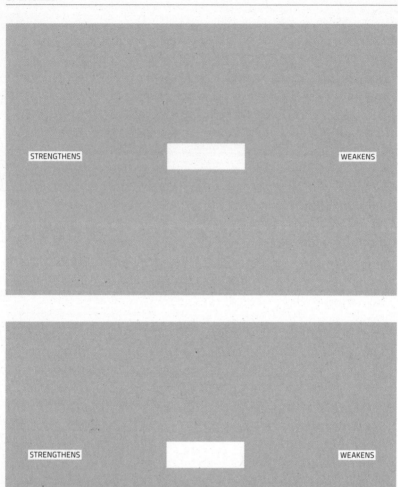

5 Implications

Thinking about some of the aspects of lived experience identified above, what kind of implications or new points of intervention could be made?

REFERENCES

1 World Bank (2010). World Bank Poverty Brief. http://go.worldbank.org/2UJWJC2XG0 [Accessed 31 January 2011].

2 Millennium Ecosystem Assessment (2005). Ecosystems and Human Well-Being: Synthesis. Washington, DC: Island Press.

3 Brewer, M., Muriel, A., Phillips, D., and Sibieta, L. (2009) Poverty and inequality in the UK: 2009. IFS Commentary. http://www.ifs.org.uk/publications/4524 [Accessed 20 February 2011].

4 UNICEF (2007), A Comprehensive Assessment of the Lives and Well-Being of Children and Adolescents in the Economically Advanced Nations. Innocenti Research Centre, Report Card 7.

5 Siddique, H. Three-quarters of non-Muslims believe Islam negative for Britain. Guardian, Monday 2 August 2010; Telegraph. "Islam associated with terrorism by public, poll shows." 7 June 2010; Townsend, M. Searchlight poll finds huge support for far right 'if they gave up violence.' Guardian, Saturday 26 February 2011.

6 Third Sector Foresight. Attitudes towards domestic poverty. Thursday 3 February 2011. http://www.3s4.org.uk/ drivers/attitudes-towards-domestic-poverty [Accessed 15 February 2011]; Hanley, T. Engaging public support for eradicating UK poverty. Joseph Rowntree Foundation, 24 September 2009. http://www.jrf.org.uk/ publications/public-support-eradicating-poverty-uk [Accessed 16 February 2011].

7 Schwartz, S. (2011). Studying Values: Personal Adventure, Future Directions. Journal of Cross-Cultural Psychology, 42(3), 307–19.

8 **Attitudes:**

Political persuasions: Caprara, G. V., Schwartz, S., Capanna, C., Vecchione, M. and Barbaranelli, C. (2006) Personality and Politics: Values, Traits, and Political Choice. Political Psychology, 27(1), 1–28. Caprara, G., Vecchione, M. and Schwartz, S. H. (2009), Mediational role of values in linking personality traits to political orientation. Asian Journal of Social Psychology, 12 (2), 82–94.

Social and environmental accountability of companies: Fukukawa, K., Shafer, W. E. and Lee, G. M. (2007). Values and attitudes toward social and environmental accountability: a study of MBA students. Journal of Business Ethics, 71 (4), 381–394.

Interests: Brickman, S. J., Miller, R.B. and McInerney, D. M. (2005). Values, interests and environmental preferences for the school context. Australian Association of Educational Research, Sydney. Sodano, S. M. (2010). Integrating work and basic values into the spherical model of interests? Journal of Vocational Behavior, 78 (1), 1–10. Sagiv, L. (2002). Vocational interests and basic values. Journal of Career Assessment, 10 (2), 233–257.

Nationalism: Roccas, S., Schwartz, S. H. and Amit, A. (2010). Personal Value Priorities and National Identification. Political Psychology, 31 (3), 2010.

Human rights: Spini, D. and Doise, W. (1998). Organising principles of involvement in human rights and their social anchoring in value priorities. European Journal of Social Psychology, 28 (4), 603–622. Cohrs, J.C., Maes, J., Moschner, B. and Kielmann, S. (2007). Determinants of human rights attitudes and behaviour: a comparison and integration of psychological perspectives. Political Psychology, 28 (4), 441–470.

Militarism & peacefulness: Cohrs, J.C., Moschner, B., Maes, J. and Kielmann, S. (2005). Personal values and attitudes toward war. Peace and Conflict: Journal of Peace Psychology, 11 (3), 293–312.

Global poverty: Doran, C.J. (2009). The role of personal values in fair trade consumption. Journal of Business Ethics, 84 (4), 549–563.

Global conflict: Fischer, R. and Hanke, K. (2009). Are societal values linked to global peace and conflict? Peace and Conflict, 15 (3), 227–248.

Concern about environmental damage: Schultz, P.W., Gouveia, VV., Cameron, L.D., Tankha, G., Schmuck, P. and Frank, M. (2005). Values and their relationship to environmental concern and conservation behaviour. Journal of Cross-Cultural Psychology, 36 (4), 457–475; Degenhardt, L. (2002). Why do people act in sustainable ways?

Results of an empirical survey of lifestyle pioneers. In P. Schmuck and P.W. Schultz, eds. Psychology of sustainable development. Dordrecht, Netherlands: Kluwer Academic Publishers, pp. 123–147. Support of environmental policies: Lieserowitz, A. (2006). Climate change risk perception and policy preferences: the role of affect, imagery and values. Climatic Change, 77, 45–72.

Sexism, racism and out-group prejudice: Hall, D. L., D. C. Matz, and W. Wood (2010, February). Why don't we practice what we preach? A meta-analytic review of religious racism. Personality and Social Psychology Review, 14 (1), 126–139; Schwartz, S. H. (2007). Universalism values and the inclusiveness of our moral universe. Journal of Cross-Cultural Psychology, 38 (6), 711–728; Davidov, E., Meuleman, B., Billiet, J. and Schmidt, P. (2008). Values and support for Immigration: a cross-country comparison. European Sociological Review, 24 (5), 583–599; Feather, N.T. (2004). Value correlates of ambivalent attitudes toward gender relations. Personality and Social Psychology Bulletin, 30 (1), 3–12; Sawyerr, O.O., Strauss, J. and Yan, J. (2005). Individual value structure and diversity attitudes: the moderating effects of age, gender, race, and religiosity. Journal of Managerial Psychology, 20 (6), 498–521;Duriez, B., Vansteenkiste, M., Soenens, B. and De Witte, H. (2007). The social costs of extrinsic relative to intrinsic goal pursuits: their relation with social dominance and racial and ethnic prejudice. Journal of Personality, 75 (4), 757–782; Roets, A., Van Hiel, C. and Cornelis, I. (2006) Does materialism predict racism? Materialism as a distinctive social attitude and a predictor of prejudice. European Journal of Personality, 20 (2), 155–168; Feather, N.T. and McKee, I.R. (2008). Values and prejudice: predictors of attitudes towards Australian Aborigines. Australian Journal of Psychology, 60 (2), 80–90.

Immigration: Davidov, E. et al. (2008). Op cit.

Gay rights: Haider-Markel, D.P. and Joslyn, M.R. (2008). Beliefs about the origins of homosexuality and support for gay rights: an empirical test of attribution theory. Public Opinion Quarterly, 72 (2), 291–310.

Punishment or rehabilitation: McKee, I. and Feather, N. (2008). Revenge, retribution, and values: Social attitudes and punitive sentencing. Social Justice Research, 21 (2), 138–163.

Big issues: Schwartz, S. H., Sagiv, L. and Boehnke, K. (2000). Worries and Values. Journal of Personality, 68 (2), 309–346.

Moral behaviour: Lan, G., M. Gowing, S. McMahon, F. Rieger, and N. King (2008). A study of the relationship between personal values and moral reasoning of undergraduate business students. Journal of Business Ethics 78 (1), 121–139.

Behaviours:
Voting: Schwartz, S. H., Caprara, G. V. and Vecchione, M. (2010). Basic Personal Values, Core Political Values, and Voting: A Longitudinal Analysis. Political Psychology, 31 (3), 421–452.

Purchasing decisions: Pepper, M., Jackson, T. and Uzzell, D. (2009). An examination of the values that motivate socially conscious and frugal consumer behaviours. International Journal of Consumer Studies, 33 (2), 126–136.

Ethical purchasing: Ibid.

Political activism: Amit, A., Roccas, S. and Meidan, M. (2010). A group just like me: The moderating role of conservation values on social projection. European Journal of Social Psychology, 40 (6), 931–945.

Altruism: Sagiv, L., Sverdlik, N. and Schwarz, N. (2011). To compete or to cooperate? Values' impact on perception and action in social dilemma games. European Journal of Social Psychology, 41 (1), 64–77. Lönnqvist, J.-E., S. Leikas, S. Paunonen, V. Nissinen, and M. Verkasalo (2006). Conformism moderates the relations between values, anticipated regret, and behavior. Personality and Social Psychology Bulletin, 32 (11), 1469–1481; Dietz, T., Kalof, L. and Stern, P. C. (2002). Gender, Values, and Environmentalism. Social Science Quarterly, 83 (1), 353–364; Milfont, T. L., J. Duckitt, and L. D. Cameron (2006). A Cross-cultural study of environmental motive concerns and their implications for proenvironmental behavior. Environment and Behavior, 38 (6), 745–767.

Diet: Baker, S., Thompson, K. E., Engelken, J. and Huntley K., (2004). Mapping the values driving organic food choice: Germany vs the UK, European Journal of Marketing, 38 (8), 995–1012; Brunsø, K., Scholderer, J. and Grunert, K. (2004). Testing relationships between values and food-related lifestyle: results from two European countries. Appetite, 43 (2), 195–205; Dreezensa, E., Martijna, C., Tenbültb, P., Koka, G. and de Vriesb, N. (2005). Food and values: an examination of values underlying attitudes toward genetically modified and organically grown food products. Appetite, 44 (1), 115–122; Homer, P. M., and Kahle, L. R. (1988). A structural equation test of the value-attitude-behavior hierarchy. Journal of Personality and Social Psychology, 54 (4), 638–646; Grønhøj, A. and J. Thøgersen (2009). Like father, like son? Intergenerational transmission of values, attitudes, and behaviours in the environmental domain. Journal of Environmental Psychology, 1 (2), 105–126.

Career: Sagiv, L. (2002). Op cit.

Volunteering: Caprara, G.V., Steca, P. (2007). Prosocial agency: The contribution of values and self-efficacy beliefs to prosocial behaviour across ages. Journal of Social and Clinical Psychology, 26 (3), 220–241.

Empathy: Silfver, M., Helkama, K., Lönnqvist, J.E. and Verkasalo, M. (2008). The relation between value priorities and proneness to guilt, shame, and empathy. Motivation and Emotion, 32 (2), 69–80.

Recycling: Thøgersen, J. (1996). Recycling and morality. A critical review of the literature. Environment and Behavior, 28 (4), 536–558; Hopper, J. R., & McCarl-Nielsen, J. (1991). Recycling as altruistic behavior. Normative and behavioral strategies to expand participation in a community recycling program. Environment and Behavior, 23 (2), 195–220.

Electricity conservation: Grønhøj, A. and J. Thøgersen (2009). Op cit.

Litter: Schultz, P.W. et al. (2005). Op cit.

Walking/cycling: Ibid.

Ecological footprints: Brown, K.W. and Kasser, T. (2005). Are psychological and ecological well-being compatible? The role of values, mindfulness and lifestyle. Social Indicators Research, 74 (2), 349–368.

9 Barr, S. (2003). Strategies for sustainability: citizens and responsible environmental behaviour. Area, 35 (3), 227–240.

10 Schwartz, S.H. (1992). Universals in the content and structure of values: theoretical advances and empirical tests in 20 countries. In M.P. Zanna, ed. Advances in Experimental Social Psychology, 25. Orlando: Academic Press, pp. 1–65; Rokeach, M. (1973). The Nature of Human Values. New York: The Free Press.

11 Ibid.

12 Ibid.

13 Ibid.; Schwartz, S.H. (1994). Are there universal aspects in the structure and contents of human values? Journal of Social Issues, 50 (4), 19–45.

14 Schwartz, S.H. (2006a). Basic human values: Theory, measurement, and applications. Revue française de sociologie, 47 (4), 249–288.

15 Schwartz, S.H. (1992). Op cit.

16 Ibid.

17 Maio, G.R., Pakizeh, A., Cheung, W.Y. and Rees, K.J. (2009). Changing, priming, and acting on values: effects via motivational relations in a circular model. Journal of Personality and Social Psychology, 97 (4), 699–715; Burgoyne, C.B. and Lea, S.E.G. (2006). Money is material. Science, 314 (5802), 1091–1092; Vohs, K.D., Mead, N.L. and Goode, M.R. (2006). The psychological consequences of money, Science, 314 (5802), 1154–1156.

18 Sheldon, K. M., Nichols, C. P., & Kasser, T. (in press). Americans recommend smaller ecological footprints when reminded of intrinsic American values of self-expression, family, and generosity. Ecopsychology.

19 Maio et al. (2009). Op cit.

20 Carney, J.K. (1986). Intrinsic Motivation and Artistic Success. Unpublished dissertation. University of Chicago; Getzels, J.W. and Csikszentmihalyi, M. (1976). The Creative Vision: A Longitudinal Study of Problem-Finding in Art. New York: Wiley.

21 Kasser, T., Ahuvia, A., Fernandez-Dols, J.M., Grouzet, F.M.E., Kim, Y., Lau, S., Ryan, R.M., Saunders, S., Schmuck, P. and Sheldon, K.M. (2005). The Structure of Goal Contents Across 15 Cultures. Journal of Personality and Social Psychology, 89 (5), 800–816.

22 Ibid.

23 Schwartz, S. H. (2006b). Basic Human Values: An Overview. Jerusalem: The Hebrew University of Jerusalem.

24 Ibid.

25 Sagiv, L. et al. (2011). Op cit; Lönnqvist, J.E. et al. (2006). Op cit; Dietz, T., Kalof, L. and Stern, P.C. (2002). Gender, Values, and Environmentalism. Social Science Quarterly, 83 (1): 353–364; Milfont, T. L., Duckitt, J. and Cameron, L. D. (2006). A Cross-Cultural study of environmental motive concerns and their implications for pro-environmental behaviour. Environment and Behavior, 38 (6), 745–767.

26 Duriez, B. et al. (2007). Op cit.

27 Hall, D.L., Matz, D.C. and Wood, W. (2010). Why don't we practice what we preach? A meta-analytic review of religious racism. Personality and Social Psychology Review, 14 (1), 126–139; Schwartz, S.H. (2007). Op cit; Davidov, E. et al (2008). Op cit; Feather, N.T. (2004). Value correlates of ambivalent attitudes toward gender relations. Personality and Social Psychology Bulletin, 30 (1), 3–12; Sawyerr, O.O., Strauss, J. and Yan, J. (2005). Individual value structure and diversity attitudes: the moderating effects of age, gender, race, and religiosity. Journal of Managerial Psychology, 20 (6), 498–521; Duriez, B. et al (2007). Op cit; Roets, A. et al. (2006). Op cit; Feather, N.T. and McKee, I.R. (2008). Op cit.

28 Milfont, T. L., Duckitt, J. and Cameron, L. D. (2006). Op cit ; Schultz, P.W. et al. (2005). Op cit; Degenhardt, L. (2002). Op cit.

29 Spini, D. and Doise, W. (1998). Op cit.

30 McHoskey, J. W. (1999). Machiavellianism, intrinsic versus extrinsic goals, and social interest: A self-determination theory analysis. Motivation and Emotion, 23 (4), 267–283.

31 Sheldon, K.M., Sheldon, M.S., and Osbaldiston, R. (2000). Prosocial values and group-assortation within an N-person prisoner's dilemma. Human Nature, 11 (4), 387–404; Sagiv, L. et al. (2011). Op cit.

32 Kasser, T. (2002). The High Price of Materialism. London: MIT Press.

33 Ibid.

34 Bardi, A. and Schwartz, S.H. (2003). Values and behavior: Strength and structure of relations. Personality and Social Psychology Bulletin, 29 (10), 1207–1220.

35 Ibid.

36 Latané, B., and Darley, J. M. (1976). Help in a crisis: Bystander response to an emergency. Morristown: General Learning Press.

37 Webster, P., and Riddell, P. (2006). The green divide: Times poll shows the gulf between words and action on the environment. The Times. 8 November 2006. Available at http://www.timesonline.co.uk/tol/news/uk/health/article 629238.ece [Accessed 5 January 2011]; Dovidio, J. F. and Gaertner, S. L. (1998). On the nature of contemporary prejudice: The causes, consequences, and challenges of aversive racism. In J. L. Eberhardt S. T. Fiske, eds. Confronting racism: The problem and the response. Thousand Oaks: Sage, pp. 3–32.

38 Maio, G. R., Olson, J. M., Allen, L. and Bernard, M. M. (2001). Addressing discrepancies between values and behavior: The motivating effect of reasons. Journal of Experimental Social Psychology, 37 (2), 104–117.

39 Maio, G. R., Hahn, U., Frost, J., and Cheung, W. (2009). Applying the value of equality unequally: Effects of value instantiations that vary in typicality. Journal of Personality and Social Psychology, 97 (4), 598–614.

40 Maio, G. R., Olson, J. M., Allen, L., and Bernard, M. M. (2001). Addressing discrepancies between values and behavior: The motivating effect of reasons. Journal of Experimental Social Psychology, 37 (2), 104–117.

41 Lönnqvist, J.E. et al. (2006). Op cit; Mellema, A. and Bassili, J. N. (1995). On the relationship between attitudes and values: exploring the moderating effects of self-monitoring and self-monitoring schematicity. Personality and Social Psychology Bulletin, 21 (9), 885–892.

42 Ajzen, I. (1991). The theory of planned behavior. Organizational Behavior and Human Decision Processes, 50 (2), 179–211.

43 Craig, S. C., Kane, J. G., and Martinez, M. D. (2002). Sometimes you feel like a nut, sometimes you don't: citizens' ambivalence about abortion. Political Psychology, 23 (2), 285–301.

44 Brewer, P. R. (2003). The shifting foundations of public opinion about gay rights. Journal of Politics, 65 (4), 1208–1220.

45 Feldman, S. (1988). Structure and consistency in public opinion: The role of core beliefs and values. American Journal of Political Science, 32 (2), 417–440.

46 Katz, I., and Hass, R.G. (1988). Racial ambivalence and American value conflict: Correlational and priming studies of dual cognitive structures. Journal of Personality and Social Psychology, 55 (6), 893–905.

47 Berndsen, M., and van der Pligt, J. (2004). Ambivalence towards meat. Appetite, 42 (1), 71–78.

48 Crandall, C. S., D'Anello, S., Sakalli, N., Lazarus, E., Wieczorkowska, G., and Feather, N. T. (2001). An attribution-value model of prejudice: Anti-fat attitudes in six nations. Personality and Social Psychology Bulletin, 27 (1), 30–37.

49 Maio, G. R., Hahn, U., Frost, J. M. and Cheung, W. (manuscript in preparation). Social values as persuasive arguments: Similar is convincing.

50 Maio, G.R. (2010). Mental Representations of Social Values. In M.P. Zanna, ed. Advances in Experimental Social Psychology, Vol. 42. Burlington: Academic Press, 2010, pp. 1–43.

51 Hüther, G. (2006). Neurobiological approaches to a better understanding of human nature and human values. The Journal for Transdisciplinary Research in Southern Africa, 2 (2), 331–343; Banerjee, R. and Dittmar, H. (2008). Individual differences in children's materialism: the role of peer relations. Personality and Social Psychology Bulletin, 31 (1), 17–31; Flouri, E. (1999). An integrated model of consumer materialism: can economic socialisation and maternal values predict materialistic attitudes in adolescents? Journal of Socio-Economics, 28 (6), 707–724; Goldberg, M.E., Gorn, G.J., Peracchio, L.A. and Bamossy, G. (2003). Understanding materialism among youth. Journal of Consumer Psychology, 13 (3), 278–288; Sheldon, K.M. and McGregor, H. (2000). Extrinsic value orientation and the tragedy of the commons. Journal of Personality, 68 (2), 383–411.

52 Sheldon, K.M. and Krieger, L.S. (2004). Does legal education have undermining effects on law students? Evaluating changes, motivation, values and well-being. Behavioral Sciences and the Law, 22 (2), 261–286.

53 Angelucci, L., Da Silva, J., Juarez, J. (2009). Values and socio-demographic factors in university students: a comparative study. Acta Colombiana de Psicología,12 (1), 151–162.

54 Soss, J. and Schram, S.F. (2007). A public transformed? Welfare reform as policy feedback. American Political Science Review, 101 (1), 111–127.

55 Ibid.; Brewer, J. and Lakoff, G. Why voters aren't motivated by a laundry list of positions on issues. Cognitive Policy Works, 2008a. Available at www.cognitivepolicyworks.com/what-wedo/cognitive-policy/why-voters-

arent-motivated-by-a-laundry-list-of-positions-on-issues [Accessed 2 April 2011]; Brewer, J. and Lakoff, G. Comparing climate proposals: a case study in cognitive policy. Cognitive Policy Works, 2008b. Available at http://www.cognitivepolicyworks.com/what-we-do/cognitive-policy/comparing-climate-proposals-a-case-study-in-cognitive-policy [Accessed 2 April 2011].

56 Schwartz, S.H. (2007). Cultural and Individual Value Correlates of Capitalism: A Comparative Analysis. Psychological Inquiry, 18(1), 52–57; Kasser, T.; Cohn, S.; Kanner, A.D. and Ryan, R.M. (2007). Some Costs of American Corporate Capitalism: A Psychological Exploration of Value and Goal Conflicts. Psychological Inquiry, 18(1):1–22.

57 Taken from responses in workshops and research base; for example: Bardi, A.; Calogero, R.M. and Mullen, B. (2008). A New Archival Approach to the Study of Values and Value—Behavior Relations: Validation of the Value Lexicon. Journal of Applied Psychology, 93 (3), 483–497; Konty, M.; Duell, B. and Joireman, J. (2006). Scared selfish: a culture of fear's values in the age of terrorism. The American Sociologist, 35 (2), 93–109; Hüther, G. (2006). Op cit; Banerjee, R. and Dittmar, H. (2008). Op cit; Flouri, E. (1999). Op cit; Goldberg, M.E. et al. (2003). Op cit; Sheldon, K.M. and McGregor, H. (2000). Op cit; Sheldon, K.M. and Krieger, L.S. (2004). Op cit; Angelucci, L. et al. (2009). Op cit; Soss, J. and Schram, S.F. (2007). Op cit; Brewer, J. and Lakoff, G. (2008a). Op cit; Brewer, J. and Lakoff, G. (2007). Op cit; Schwartz, S.H. (2007). Op cit; Kasser, T. et al. (2007). Op cit.

58 Wade, M.D., Liu, L.A. and Vacek, J. (2011). Values and Upward Influence Strategies in Transition: Evidence From the Czech Republic. Journal of Cross-Cultural Psychology, 42 (2), 288–306.

59 Ibid.

60 Svallfors, S. (2010). Policy feedback, generational replacement, and attitudes to state intervention: Eastern and Western Germany, 1990–2006. European Political Science Review, 2 (1), 119–135.

61 Addison, P. (1975). The Road to 1945. London: Cape.

62 Becker, A. E. (2004, December). Television, disordered eating, and young women in Fiji: Negotiating body image and identity during rapid social change. Culture, Medicine and Psychiatry, 28 (4), 533–559.

63 Verkasalo, M., Goodwin, R., and Bezmenova, I. (2006). Value change following a major terrorist incident: Finnish adolescent and student values before and after 11th September 2001. Journal of Applied Social Psychology, 36 (1), 144–160; Frink, D. D., Rose, G. M., and Canty, A. L. (2004). The effects of values on worries associated with acute disaster: A naturally occurring quasi-experiment. Journal of Applied Social Psychology, 34 (1), 85–107; Goodwin, R. and Gaines, S. (2009). Terrorism perception and its consequences following the 7th July 2005 London bombings. Behavioral Sciences of Terrorism and Political Aggression, 1 (1), 50–65.

64 Deneulin, S. (2009). Advancing human development: Values, groups, power and conflict. WeD Working Paper 09/49. Bath, UK: University of Bath/Wellbeing in Developing Countries Research Group.

65 Rokeach, M. (1979). Change And Stability In American Value Systems 1968–1971. In M. Rokeach, ed. Understanding Human Values: Individual and Societal. New York: The Free Press/ Simon and Schuster, pp. 129–147.

66 Arat, Y. (1998). Feminists, Islamists, and Political Change in Turkey. Political Psychology, 19 (1),117–131.

67 See, for example, Darnton, A. and Kirk, M. (2011). Finding Frames: New ways to engage the UK public in global poverty. Available at http://www.findingframes.org/report.htm [Accessed 10 April 2011] or www.valuesand frames.org/downloads; G. Lakoff, et al. (2004). Don't Think of an Elephant: Know Your Values and Frame the Debate. Vermont: Chelsea Green Publishing Company; Cienki, A. (2007). Frames, idealised cognitive models, and domains. In Geeraerts, D and H. Cuyckens. The Oxford Handbook of Cognitive Linguistics, pp. 170–187, Oxford: OUP; Fillmore, C (1985) Frames and the semantics of understanding, in Quaderni di Semantica, 6, 222–254.

68 Lau, R.R. and Schlesinger, M. (2005). Policy frames, metaphorical reasoning, and support and support for public policies. Political Psychology, 26 (1), 77–114.

69 Other examples discussed in: Shenkar-Osorio, A., 2010. You Say Tax Cut... Let's Call the Whole Thing Off. The Huffington Post, 2010. Available at http://www.huffingtonpost.com/anat-shenkerosorio/you-say-tax-cutlets-call-_b_794521.html [Accessed 10 February 2011].

70 Darnton, A. and Kirk, M. (2011). Op cit.

71 For example, see: Schwartz, S. H. (2006a). Basic human values: Theory, measurement, and applications. Revue française de sociologie, 47 (4), 249–288; McHoskey, J. W. (1999). Op cit; Crompton, T. Common Cause: The case for working with our cultural values, 2010. Available online at: http://assets.wwf.org.uk/downloads/common_cause_report.pdf [Accessed 4 January 2011]; Mixing with out-groups: Sagiv, L. and Schwartz, S.H. (1995). Value priorities and readiness for out-group social contact. Journal of Personality and Social Psychology, 69 (3), 437–448.

72 Wilkinson, R. and Pickett, K. (2009). The Spirit Level: Why More Equal Societies Almost Always Do Better. London: Penguin.

73 Mills, J., Polivy, J., Herman, C. P., and Tiggemann, M. (2002). Effects of exposure to thin media images: evidence of self-enhancement among restrained eaters. Personality and Social Psychology Bulletin, 28 (12), 1687–1699; Fredrickson, B. L., Roberts,T., Noll, S. M., Quinn, D. M., and Twenge, J.M. (1998). That swimsuit becomes you: sex differences in self-objectification, restrained eating, and math performance. Journal of Personality and Social Psychology, 75 (1), 269–284; Krassas, N. R., Blauwkamp, J. M., and Wesselink, P. (2003). "Master your Johnson": Sexual rhetoric in Maxim and Stuff magazines. Sexuality & Culture, 7 (3), 98–119.

74 American Psychological Association (2007). Report of the APA Task Force on the Sexualisation of Girls. Executive summary available online at: http://www.apa.org/pi/women/programs/girls/report.aspx [Accessed 20 March 2011].

75 Darnton, A. and Kirk, M. (2011). Op cit.

76 Bardi, A. and Schwartz, S.H. (2003). Op cit.

77 See Maio, G.R. (2010). Op cit.

78 For example, Bardi, A. and Schwartz, S.H. (2003). Op cit.

79 www.europeansocialsurvey.org

80 www.worldvaluessurvey.org

81 Gibbons, R. (1997). Incentives and Careers in Organizations. In: Kreps, D. and Wallis, K., eds. Advances in Economic Theory and Econometrics, Vol.2. Cambridge: Cambridge University Press; Prendergast, C. (1999). The Provision of Incentives in Firms. Journal of Economic Literature, 37(1), 7–63; Lazear, E. (2000). Performance Pay and Productivity. American Economic Review, 90(5), 1346–1361.

82 Titmuss, R. (1970). The Gift Relationship. London: Allen and Unwin.

83 Gneezy, U. and Rustichini, A. (2000a). A Fine is a Price. Journal of Legal Studies, 29(1), 1–17.

84 Frey, B.S. and Gotte, L. (1999). Does Pay Motivate Volunteers? Institute for Empirical Economic Research, University of Zurich, Working Paper 7.

85 Gneezy, U. and Rustichini, A. (2000b). Pay Enough or Don't Pay at All. Quarterly Journal of Economics, 115(3), 791–810.

86 Frey, B.S. and Oberholzer-Gee, F. (1997). The Cost of Price Incentives: An Empirical Analysis of Motivation Crowding-Out. The American Economic Review, 87 (4), 746–755.

87 See, for instance, Shrubsole, G. (2011). Forthcoming chapter. In ResPublica, eds. Beyond Carbon [forthcoming].